PRAISE FOR *CARDINAL SIN*:

"I saw Keith O'Brien as a credible charismatic Cardinal, orthodox but with a liberal streak. How wrong was I. The cosy Catholic hierarchical system made it easy for him to be the fraud and hypocrite he was. It protected him as it has protected many other predatory gay clerics who masquerade not just as celibate heterosexuals but as teachers and preachers of the very dysfunctional Church teaching on homosexuality that conduces to homophobia. Without courageous whistleblowers like the author Brian Devlin we would never know the extent of the corruption that facilitated O'Brien and others like him. This book is written by a loving critic not a sensationalist. It hopes for healing."

MARY MCALEESE

D0916649

"*Cardinal Sin* is an important book because it is written by an insider with intimate knowledge of the church and its failings. The exposure of Cardinal Keith O'Brien shook the wall of the Catholic hierarchy internationally, and the reverberations were far reaching. In a turbulent time, Brian Devlin was brave and steadfast, never losing sight of Keith O'Brien's humanity, or his own. He focused on the heart of the struggle: not the exposure of a single frail man but the cleansing of a powerful church which had become a two-headed monster, facing one way in public and another in private."

CATHERINE DEVENEY. WRITER AND JOURNALIST

Brian Devlin was ordained a Catholic Priest in Edinburgh in 1985. Once the announcement that Keith O'Brien would be ordained as his Archbishop, he left the priesthood to work with heroin users in Leith. After a period in AIDS prevention, Brian gained management experience in the NHS, ending up as Director of PR. He now holds various charitable and voluntary roles.

CARDINAL
SIN

Challenging power abuse in the
Catholic Church

BRIAN DEVLIN

columba
BOOKS

First published in 2021 by

 **columba**BOOKS

Block 3b, Bracken Business Park,
Bracken Road, Sandyford,Dublin 18, D18 K277
www.columbabooks.com

ISBN: 978-1-78218-3846

Set in Linux Libertine 11.5/16 and Cinzel
Book design by Maria Soto | Columba Books
Cover design by Alba Esteban | Columba Books

Cover image: Cardinal Keith O'Brien, archbishop of Saint Andrews and
Edinburgh attends a mass held by Pope Benedict XVI in St. Peter's Basilica
on February 19, 2012 in Vatican City. Photography by Franco Origlia /
Stringer. Source: Getty Images Europe

Printed by L&C, Poland

This book is dedicated to Caroline Thomson
– my wise counsellor, my friend
and my bringer of laughter.
Sorely missed and never forgotten.

CONTENTS

PROLOGUE

My original intention had been to tell a curious tale. It was to recount the story of what it was like to be a whistle-blower in the Catholic Church in Scotland – one of a small group of four men who went public about our experiences of abuse at the hands of Cardinal Keith O'Brien. Having had a front-row seat when the story was made public, I was up close to the reactions of those in power – people intimate with the Pope himself – and others who had varying degrees of authority in the Catholic church.

That's what I wrote originally, or what I thought I had written. What I ended up with, however, was not the book I truly wanted to write. It became clear that what I had produced was a book of anger, of hurt and of unresolved issues. The more I wrote, the angrier I appeared to be. Someone read what I had written and said that it seemed as though I hated the Catholic Church. That shocked me. It was like a slap in the face. I don't have it in me to hate the Church. Criticise it, dissent from its more lurid teachings, certainly. Catholicism is a defining part of who I am. It is as much a part of me as my childhood is. It has helped to shape me.

I am a Catholic, albeit a non-practising one, and I am a former priest who does not seek a dispensation from the vows I made at ordination for reasons that will become clear later. This means that I have no active position in the

Church. That's a sadness to me but one that I have come to accept. But that does not in the least make me feel less affection and loyalty for the organisation and a deeply held view that I want to help it to be everything it should be – a place of love, forgiveness, transparency and sacrifice.

I did not realise just how much I was affected by the consequences of what Keith O'Brien did to me and by what the ecclesiastical hierarchy continue to do to the Church I devoted my young life to. The way they dealt with us – victims and whistle-blowers – reflected the present domineering style of governance within Catholicism. It was painful. That may explain why my anger and frustration was so negatively expressed.

On hearing those views about my angry tone, I made a decision to rethink very deeply about what I wanted to say. My story, the front-row seat one is interesting, I think, and I will tell it all. However, a mere recounting of what happened is not enough. I feel, very strongly, that theologically sound structural change is required to make the Church more authentically aligned to the message of its founder, Jesus of Nazareth. In short, Catholicism needs another reformation.

I want the Church to learn from the O'Brien case and other cases like it. But that will take a great deal of effort. Currently, there are very real perils for Catholicism, and these are due to this fundamentally loving and responsive institution being led by men who, often with good intentions, are in the wrong place. Also the billion or so lay people, many of whom are trapped and disempowered, being in the wrong place too.

So, as well as telling my tale, this book raises lots of questions. Some of them big and some of them not so big. I hope that it will play its part in the discussions that Catholics and others are having across the world as to the future of their Church.

One fundamental question is: why do low standards of behaviour, cruelty and abuse continue to happen with such regularity in the Catholic Church and, when they do, why does it matter to people so much? It's not as though the Church has a monopoly on malfeasance. Many institutions harbour and nestle bad and sometimes illegal behaviour. But the level of hurt and pain in the Catholic Church is notably enduring and felt deeply.

A search for an answer to my question could reasonably begin back in the mists of time where, as early as 381 years after Jesus' death, Church leaders, in a grand affair in Constantinople, declared their creed to be: 'In one, holy, catholic and apostolic Church; we acknowledge one baptism for the remission of sins; we look for the resurrection of the dead; and the life of the world to come. Amen.'

Amen, indeed.

It is quite a claim. I suppose it should come as no great shock, if that is your belief, that when low standards of behaviour and abuse happen in the one, holy, catholic and apostolic Church, people are going to feel it deeply.

The Church, Catholics are taught, is a creation and a manifestation of the divine. If the 'holy' Church proves itself only to be holy on the outside, then nothing as simple as a campaign will fix it. #HolyAgain won't work.

I refuse to believe, however, despite its propensity towards self-harm, that the Church is a hopeless case with nothing left to offer the world now. I hope to demonstrate that, while it is in serious jeopardy, there are actions that it can take to heal itself and to regain the trust of the people for whom it is central. This will not happen without real reform and a true sense of purpose in the years and decades ahead. It needs more than a cosmetic shift. The paradigm has to change dramatically. If there is a will among the Church hierarchy and the people in the pews, then it *can* be the true mirror of Christ's vision it claims to be. But does such a will exist, and what would such a reform look like? In the latter part of the book I have made some reflections which I believe, if followed, would help make the Catholic Church the body it wants to be and not the irrelevant relic it risks becoming.

For my own part, I have made three reflective journeys since I happened across Keith O'Brien, the Spiritual Director of the seminary where I studied in 1978. One of these journeys was the years that I spent travelling into and out of the Catholic priesthood and what happened to me along the way. The second is a journey into the curious, bewildering and often intimidating world of the official Church 'dealing with' my complaint about the inappropriate, and ultimately spiritually destructive, behaviour perpetrated by Keith O'Brien.

The third journey is the aftermath: what I have learned about myself and the Church. In some senses this has been the hardest journey to make. I'm a doubter and a questioner, by nature. I do not envy any man or woman certainty in their faith. That certainty intimidates me somewhat. It often irritates me too. Nor am I an admirer of certain atheism. It can be as blind and as strident as religious fundamentalism. I inhabit one certainty. I am certain that I don't know.

You will learn that I was fond of Keith O'Brien when he was my Spiritual Director in Drygrange seminary until he abused the trust I had in him. He was many things to me: a friend, a mentor, a funny man, but, more than anything else, he was a teacher.

He taught me that I do, in fact, have certainty about one fundamental premise of the Christian tradition. That is the premise of 'original sin'. This is something I learned from a very close friend, quite late on in my life, and during the process of writing this book. You don't need to be religious to believe in original sin. You just need to be human. It is our brand. It can also be the source of our compassion when addressing issues that have hurt us. We are, each and every one of us, works-in-progress. Our journey through life, if we are at all reflective, teaches us that we have much to learn in our humble state of being.

PART ONE

THE LONG TREK

1

A DAY LIKE NO OTHER

I remember vividly my reaction as the message dropped into my inbox. "Do you find yourself wondering how he is?"

It was from Catherine Deveney, the journalist who had just broken the story about the sexual hypocrisy of Cardinal Keith O'Brien a few days previously, the story which was to throw the Catholic Church into a massive crisis, and which shook it to its core. It was a murky story, one full of betrayal, hurt and carelessness. It was a story not just about the fall from grace of one man, but of the cynicism and neglect of the entire governing structure of the Church itself.

Ultimately though, at the story's heart, lay a man. Someone who had lived his life within the confines of the institution that protected and defined him. Keith O'Brien, *Cardinal* Keith O'Brien, was the visible face of Catholicism in Scotland. I did wonder how he was.

A photo had been printed in one of the papers of him sitting at, I guess, his desk. Grey, old, bemused, hurt, cornered and humiliated. Gone now was the sureness, the thundering authority with which he held others to account. Instead, what was left was a broken man.

O'Brien had walked the stage in Scotland with certainty. He was at ease in the company of civic society's big beasts. He had a charismatic presence that meant he did not have to seek out attention. People came to him, they sought him out. They wanted his opinion. They might not always agree with it, but if Catholicism and Catholics had to be delivered for whatever cause, O'Brien had to be heard, and heard well.

The thing is though, some of the things he ended up saying were the defining factors in my decision to play a leading part in exposing him. It wasn't because he was an actively gay man living and ministering in the Catholic Church. Not even because he was a gay cardinal. There are plenty like him. No. The decision that I took in exposing him was what he *said* about others as well as what he *did* to others.

There was a line in O'Brien's last will and testament that was read out at his funeral mass 'I ask forgiveness of all I have offended in this life.' O'Brien didn't just 'offend' people. By his actions and words he bludgeoned them. He used his power and he cynically and without any concern for their well-being threw them in the dust. He left them empty and choking. At the same time he lived a life of such audacious hypocrisy I am left wondering why people who knew him, and knew of his behaviour, tolerated it, embraced it and colluded with it.

Why was it left to others to point out that this emperor, all too frequently, had no clothes on? I think I've found the answer.

* * *

I am just ordinary.

An only child of Irish parents, I spent most of my youth in the 1960s and 70s in a small village in Fife in Scotland called

Charlestown. It was a lovely place to grow up in. It was also the sort of village where it was important not to think too highly of yourself; not to have any thoughts in your head that you were, or one day may become, 'somebody'.

Being ordinary, being 'naebody special', was a survival technique in many ways. We were the only practising Catholics in the village at the time to my knowledge, and after I received my first Holy Communion in the distant Catholic primary school, I was sent to the nearby State primary school that served my village. Those were the days when tribal loyalties were part of our lived experience as a family. Tribes mattered then more than they seem to now.

Since I was a baby, I had suffered from chronic ear infections. I was pumped full of antibiotics as an infant and they rotted my teeth. My ears constantly discharged – first the right one, then the left one. Eventually I was sent to the Sick Children's Hospital in Edinburgh to have them operated on. I still remember it all.

A queue of trembling children, holding their mummies' hands, snaked its way up to the Sister in charge of the ward. She asked the name of the child, confirmed the type of operation, and told the mummy when her son or daughter would be discharged.

Name please?

This is Beth Aitkenhead.

Yes, Beth. We'll be taking your Adenoids out.

Yes, Sister.

You should be ready to go home in three days. Stop crying, child!

Name?

William Pearson, Sister, my laddie.

William. Yes I see here you've had a sore throat. Your tonsils will be removed on Friday the day after tomorrow and you should be ready to go home on Monday.

I was listening to this. I was around seven years old and had never been away from my mother's side since I was born. The thought of three or four days away from her was unimaginable to me then.

I was already weeping when we approached the Sister in her dark blue uniform and her frilly white cap. I hid behind my mother's legs so that I didn't have to see this cruel yellow-toothed woman, who was going to take me away from my mummy.

What's his name?

This is Brian Devlin, Sister.

My mother swung me round in front of her and dug her hands into my collar bones to stop me darting away.

I have an Anthony Devlin here, not a Brian.

Somewhere in my mind, I glimpsed a crack to freedom. It was all a mistake. I was going home with my mummy and another wee boy would take my place.

Ha, ha, ha, Anthony Devlin!

No that's him, Sister. His name is Anthony Brian Devlin. But we call him Brian.

I looked up at my mother. What was she making stories up like that for?

Brian, then. You've been having trouble with your ears, Brian?

I nodded. Tears fell silently down my cheeks.

You've to get your right Mastoid bone removed. You'll be with us for between six to eight weeks.

It took a few seconds to explode from my tiny pigeon-chest. The scream of pain and fear and ache came from somewhere I had not known existed. I was a child. The concept of time was just forming in me. But I remember still the weight of terror, and the sense of smallness and demolition that went through my child's body. I cried for days and days. I cried when my Mummy and Daddy left me. I cried when I woke the next day and they weren't there. I cried when, the day before my operation I wasn't given anything to eat. I cried the morning of the operation when I was wrapped tightly in a strange white blanket, like the filling in a sausage roll. A child mummified, shrieking in terror as they lifted me onto the stinking black leather trolley and wheeled me to the operating theatre. I looked up and saw lights and patterns on the roof whisking by overhead. I saw the brown damp patches, and the cartoon characters someone had thought would cheer a petrified child: Mickey, Minnie, Pluto.

The face looked down at me. A man in a mask. He spoke to me, but I couldn't hear him. The noises, and the atrocious smells of disinfectant, and medicine, and strange people. The man in the mask had something in his hand, black and rubber. The smell, and the feel of it being pushed over my mouth and nostrils. Then the gas, sickening, stealing my breath.

The weeks passed, and as they did I learned and trusted the routine. My mum heroically came to visit me on every single visiting day, carrying comics and toys. Those visits from our village in Fife involved train and bus journeys and many miles of walking in all weathers during the week when my dad was working.

Operating days were Monday, Wednesday and Friday. The routine was always the same. Starved the night before, the children woke and showered or bathed. When they came back to their bed it had been stripped of its normal sheets. Now a woollen blanket was folded on the bed. On top of that was a thin white paper hat with an elastic edge to it. The nurses folded the girl or boy into the blanket. They were given tablets to swallow to make them drowsy. Many couldn't swallow the tablets and would splutter and cry. The hats were put on. Slowly the silent procession of steel trolleys with their black leather cushions would come and take the children away.

I watched first in fascination and then soon with boredom, as this relentless hushed choreography played out before me. The children would come back after half an hour or so, blood dripping from their faces and mopped by nurses. Sometimes I was the only child awake in the vast ward. I watched from my bed, my own head swaddled in bandages. After a while, in silence I would walk down to the playroom and got the pick of the best toys. As the children woke up, one by one, they would whimper like frightened kittens and then they would cry out in shock as the pain hit them.

After my stay in hospital my mum, (I think it was about then that I stopped calling them mummy and daddy), and I used to have to make the trip every two weeks to Edinburgh from our village to see the surgeon who operated on me.

Edinburgh was miles away – a bus to Dunfermline station, the excitement of the train to Edinburgh across the Forth Bridge. I always clambered over to the side closest to the new road bridge. My dad built it, you see.

Me and another couple of Irish lads, Brian, he used to say.

My dad built that bridge, I'd say, pointing over to it to any passengers next to me. They'd smile and nod.

The doctor took a look at both my ears. Something now appeared to be up with the left ear.

We'll need him in to take a look at that.

By then I wasn't bothered. My mum and the doctor talked away, but I didn't pay any attention to them. As long as they were just going to 'take a look' and not give me an operation. I'd actually enjoyed the experience of the hospital by the time my incarceration was up. I'd created my own world from my bed near the nurses' station.

The second visit wasn't nearly as traumatic as the first one. I was known to everyone. I was a year older. The Sister waved me through. No need to queue.

That's your bed there, Brian.

Next to the nurses, Sister?

That's right. Next to the nurses.

My old bed.

I seem to remember my mum and dad were keen to get away a bit early in the visiting time. To be honest I wasn't that bothered. I had a bag of comics, a new set of Hot Wheels cars, a pack of cards, a track suit and I had my pals, the nurses, to get to know again.

So we'll get off home now.

See. You. Day. After. Tomorrow. I mouthed to them through the window of the playroom overlooking the car park. Maybe my breath had hidden my words from them? The car turned and exited.

I walked back to my bed. The bag of comics and the cars

were in the hollow where I had lain earlier. I wandered round my bed and looked at my name on the temperature chart. Anthony Brian Devlin. The name I was to be called underlined. Then my eye was drawn to the tape on the end of the bed. There were the words in blue pen '2nd Mastoid Removal Left Ear'. The following months probably formed me into the shaking insecure boy and then man I was to become.

Following these operations, which surgically were a big deal, nothing much changed with my ears in terms of my daily life. They still became infected. They still discharged.

But two things had irrevocably changed in me. One psychological, and one physical. Psychologically I changed from being a fairly happy - go - lucky, trusting wee child, to someone who had a constant anxiety about the world around him. I checked things, and rechecked them. I always said goodnight to my mum and dad. They had to answer precisely: "I'll see you in the mornin'". If they didn't say those words, then I knew that they would likely die overnight, and I would be left on my own. This anxiety, mixed with mild Obsessive Compulsive behaviour, has followed me throughout my life. Its power has peaked and wained. But it has always been there. It always will be there.

The second change was that I became, over time, deafened in both ears. Whether it was as a result of the operations or the recurring infections, or both, I don't know. I had a modicum of hearing in one ear. But hardly any of real consequence. I would sit with my ear pressed up against the television, with the volume on full. Of course, that meant I couldn't actually see the screen, so sometimes I arranged a mirror so that I could see the reflection.

Being the only Catholic in my small village and primary school, and also being the only deaf kid, meant that I was the constant centre of unwanted mocking and scrutiny.

After a time, I was to become almost completely deaf. Eventually, a hearing aid for one ear helped a bit. It was a tin box, about the size of a packet of cigarettes and lay on my chest, suspended by a ribbon of some type. An orange wire connected the aid to a mould that went into my ear. Primitive now, but a game changer for me then. Of course, it marked me out as someone even more different. I wanted to sink into the background. But I couldn't.

Around this time, a running war between largely Catholic nationalists and Protestant unionists erupted in Northern Ireland. British soldiers were killed by IRA bombs. Many of them were Scottish. Those times were described as 'the Troubles'. An understatement, if ever there was one.

It seemed to my childish brain as if all that was wrong with Ireland and the Irish was focused on Irish Catholics who lived in Scotland. Our name was Devlin. We were Irish, even though I was born and raised in Scotland. We were Catholic, and I was sometimes called an 'Irish Catholic bastard' by my wee pals.

Being an 'Irish Catholic bastard' was a tough enough gig. The thing that made it tougher was that Catholicism seemed so dark and gloomy to me. Even later, as a priest myself, I would sometimes look at the children in the pews beside their mums and dads and I so wanted to say, 'It's a lovely sunny day. Why don't you go out and play? Don't be cooped up in here. This is my job. I *have* to be here. But you? Go and have fun'. I didn't, of course.

Being ten years old and going to St Margaret's Church in Dunfermline every Sunday, while all of my Protestant friends were out playing football or watching television, felt like such a waste of a busy wee boy's time. I dreaded the church building itself with its cold grey stone and hard pews. The giant wooden crucifix with Jesus pinned to it alarmed me. The confessional, which I had to attend every fortnight, was like the inside of our airing cupboard at home which I had turned into a cosy den: hot, dark and silent. I would never have believed that some years later in that same church I would be lying prostrate at the foot of the altar, dressed in a white robe, while a litany of prayers to the saints in heaven would be sung, as I was being ordained a priest.

My parents both loved and cared for me. I loved them back. I wasn't beaten or abused. Far from it. But I was an anxious wee boy. I wore dread in the same way that other children wore a smile, and I was always afraid that, inevitably, disaster was going to hit me flat in the face. My mum and dad would die, and I would be lost and alone in the world. I knew that if I stepped out of line, even once, I would be punished. By whom? How? I didn't know.

As a child, I was always an outsider looking in. I looked in on the Catholic Church, and its boring routine. I looked in on my pals in the village and at school. They would play with me but still called me a 'Catholic bastard' when we fell out. I looked in on people speaking to me, while I struggled like an aged auntie to hear them, and responding with 'Eh? What did you say?' until they yelled back their answer. Or worse, they would mutter 'It disnae matter' and walk away, heads shaking.

There was another thing I looked in on with my pals: sex.

I have no memory of sex being discussed in my house in a formative way, ever. I know that it sounds preposterous now, but I did not know the basics of human reproduction until my early twenties. Even then, I'd say I was sketchy about the finer details. What I remember was the 'dangerousness' of it all. Its ability to destroy and lead a wee Catholic boy into sin. 'Getting a girl pregnant' and masturbation were two of the biggest sins it was possible to commit. This was drummed into me. The allure of sex, and the dangers of it, befuddled my mind. I had an overwhelming desire to run from it, from the shame and the consequences it would bring. I shudder, as well as smile, to myself as I recollect some of the excesses of my childish sexual misadventures.

My mother, like many women of her time, liked her catalogues. She'd send away for the latest crimplene number, decide she didn't want it and send it back. It was a kind of consumer ping pong match. The crimplene batted back and forth between the house and the catalogue company.

One day, alone, I was flicking through one of the many catalogues, a Kay's Club one if my memory serves me. That's when my epiphany happened. The page fell open at women in their pants and bras. Line after line of women in their pants. And corsets! My God. I had never in my life seen so many women practically naked.

There were women standing in their living rooms, in their bedrooms, walking up stairs, washing the dishes, doing the hoovering, all in their knickers smiling at me. I thought I was going to pass out. This was huge. This was a miracle - women had knickers and pants and corsets and bras, big enormous bras that lifted and separated their tits and made them pointy like big gigantic pencils and they were all there on the page in front of me. Their nipples staring me out like a cat would stare out a rabbit before devouring it.

My palms began to sweat. I was on my own in the living room, but I knew that *somehow* I was under observation. I turned the page of the catalogue. Now they were no longer in their white knickers. No. Every colour under the sun. Smiling with big bright red lips and swept back hair. These were not women that I had ever seen before. These were catalogue sex women, and my pinkie knew it.

(Oh. By the way 'pinkie' was what we called my penis. It was in a time when 'penis' would be too posh a word to use.) For the very first time in my life I felt it move.

It felt like it was taking on a life of its own. In my own house, in my own living room, my own pinkie, inside my own pants was beginning to stir. I could feel it fill up. I slammed the catalogue shut and darted to the toilet.

I ran past my mum.

Are you alright, Brian? What's the matter with ye?

Nuhin. Ahm just goin to the toilet.

I locked the snib on the door and pulled my trousers and pants down. To get a good look I took my dad's shaving mirror down and settled it on the side of the bath. (Me and mirrors.) I squatted, like a Sumo wrestler, in front of it. My pinkie was enormous. It was now Pinkie with a capital 'P'. Swollen. The catalogue sex women had done this to me.

I tentatively reached down to lift it up. Then I saw that my reflected fingers were enormous and bloated too. That's when I noticed that it was the mirror my mum had got at the market for my dad. The fancy one: two sided - one normal and one magnified. I quickly swished the mirror round to the normal view. Much smaller.... Much, much smaller. But bigger than normal, and waving at me like a drunk man swaying home from the pub.

I sat on the toilet and thought about what had happened. My pinkie (lower case again) had a mind of its own. The sex women in the catalogue in their underwear wanted me. They wanted me. But I was eleven and I was afraid.

Brian, your tea's out, my mum called.

Aye.

I was more quiet than usual that evening. The catalogue lay on the edge of the settee where I'd left it. It was like a living thing. As the draft blew in through the side of the windows and it flickered its pages. To me it was taking a breath. My dad and I watched nature programmes. There was one about big fish that just sat on the bottom of the ocean, with their mouths always open, never moving. Eventually a stupid wee fish would think it was a cave or something and swim right into the big fish's mouth, which snapped shut. That Kay's Club catalogue was lying in wait for me. Ready to draw me in, and then force feed me gussets and suspenders and knickers.

I did my homework and, when told to go to bed, for once, I didn't ask for 'just ten more minutes'.

G'night. See you in the mornin'?

See you in the mornin'

See you in the morning. Say your prayers.

I climbed into my bed. Next came my routine that no-one knew about. My prayers. I had a list of people I had to pray for. Each one got a single Hail Mary. On the list were: mum, dad, Nana, Auntie Beezie, Aunty Maura, the 'wee Black babies' in Africa, the communists, Sheena - my dog, (for the repose of her soul), Lucky the goldfish RIP (via toilet bowl). The problem was, if I deviated from the list, or forgot anyone on it, I had to go back and repeat the lot. Otherwise, obviously, they would die and I would be to blame. I couldn't just add a Hail Mary for the one I thought I had forgotten. I had to do the whole routine. Sometimes five or six times until exhaustion overtook my anxiety and I fell asleep. If I was awake, I had to say the prayer that haunted my dreams every night:

"Mathew, Mark, Luke and John
God Bless the bed that I lie on.
If I should die before I wake
I pray The Lord my soul to take."

My last waking thought was the possibility of my death.

That night I drifted off. I slept fitfully. I dreamed of women and their knickers. I dreamed that all the women on the service bus going up the town, with their message bags, didn't have any blouses on. Their big Fife women breasts juddering in their pointy bras. Then the bus conductress came swaying down the back of the bus where I sat. She had a Playtex girdle and purple lace pants on. Her lips were blood red. She moved her ticket machine, and my eyes were in line with her crotch.

A half to the Lower Bus station please, I stammered.

She looked at me. She smiled and I noticed a smear of her lipstick on her front teeth.

That'll be two and a half new pence, young man.

I woke in the morning as usual. But it wasn't as usual. There was a curious smell in my room. It smelt a bit like the Vim my mum cleaned the bath with. My pyjama bottoms were stuck to my skin round my belly and my pinkie. It was like the paste we used at school to make papier-mâché figures out of. Dry and cardboardy. I lay still for a while. What had happened? Had I peed the bed? Well no, I'd be soaking. I got up and looked down at the sheet. There was a grey stain about the size of a saucer.

Mum, I roared. MUM. MUUUUUM! Something's happened to me.

She rushed, pink faced and breathless from taking the stairs two at a time, into the room. I was standing now in my creased and cardboardy pyjamas looking at the stained sheet. She didn't say anything. Just lifted the sheet off and told me to go and get ready for school.

That night, when I came home, not a word was spoken about what had happened. We had our tea in front of the telly. Crossroads Motel.

I did my homework. I went out to play in the back garden and forgot all about the sex ladies from the catalogue.

My respite didn't last for long though.

The gang that I hang out with were all around the same age as me. We played football during all weathers, again and again. But some of our number stumbled, or fumbled, upon another distraction: 'nude books'. They were frequently discarded in the jaggiest, thorniest bushes around the village. That was no deterrent to hormonal wee laddies.

We would gather in the alpha boy's battered old shed, about six of us, and he would read from a nudie mag that he had found somewhere. It would be a tale of a young virgin bride and the first night of her honeymoon. Then he would pass round the picture of the bride in her white wedding dress, legs splayed, and lipstick smeared over her mouth. This was a step up from the catalogue alright. These women never even bothered with knickers and bras. This was a whole different set of dilemmas. Was looking bad? Was taking part in the dirty talk... was that sinful?

The no masturbation rule was branded into my mind. Scenes of misery, of my mum and dad's tears as I would be carted off to that place where they put wee Catholic boys that allowed themselves a moment of pleasure.

I came to dread going to bed because I knew when I woke in the morning, I would face the shame and silent disapproval of semen-stained sheets and pyjamas. My dream world became my enemy. I'd fall asleep after doing my paper round in the evening. Blam. I'd dose off in the back of the car going to visit my granny in Perth. Blam. I'd look too long at the lady doing the shake and vac advert before going to bed. Blam. Valerie Singleton. Blam. The one from Magpie. Blam Blam. Yvonne Goolagong. Don't get me started on her. It was like a circus trick I had inadvertently discovered. Move on Robert Brothers circus, and your trapeze artists, and your boxing kangaroo. May we introduce you to 'Nocturnal Emission Boy'?! There is no end to his magic. As if from nowhere, he produces the juices.

'Look, mum and dad, no hands!'

They didn't believe me though. The no hands bit. They didn't believe me. But it was true.

My parents thought it best that, when the time came, I

should be wrenched away from my pals to attend St Columba's RC High School in Dunfermline. It was a nice enough school, with the usual mix of nurture and psychopathy amongst the staff that secondary education seemed to attract in those days.

It was traditional at the end of the school year that staff arranged to take their classes on a field trip. For those like me in fourth year, the trips tended to be universities or colleges, so that pupils could try to gauge what their future academic interests might be. Given my frequent visits to the Fife hospitals because of my ears, I had vague notions of nursing or dealing with x-rays – but nothing specific.

We were in a chemistry class, where I was mucking around at the back, being a no-hoper in that subject, when the teacher announced that in a few weeks he'd be taking a busload of us to visit a police training college in the Borders. Any volunteers? Of course, I put my hand up along with some others and thought no more about it. I didn't want to be a policeman: I knew that already, but it was a day away from school.

I can't remember exactly when it was that I learned that I had misheard where we were to visit, and it was actually a priests', not a police, training college.

The bus was full of pupils, a few staff, and the local curate who was also the school chaplain. It was a warm summer's day and the air in the bus smelled of egg and spring onion sandwiches, which had already been eaten by the time we got to Rosyth, just a few miles into our journey. John Lennon's 'Imagine' was playing from someone's cassette player to the annoyance of the curate, who said it was heretical. Soon, we had the full gamut of mid-1970s pop music: ELO, Showaddywaddy and the Bay City Rollers.

As the bus wound its way round Edinburgh and on to the A68 towards the Borders, it was noticeable how the countryside changed. Away from industrial Fife and craggy Edinburgh, the landscape was softer, calmer. I noticed that the soil in the fields was a reddish, almost rust, colour. Shortly after the villages of Lauder and Earlston, the bus slowed and turned to the left. This was to be my first sight of St Andrew's College, Drygrange – the seminary that was to be my home for six years.

It was one of those summer days when the sun was high in the sky. You knew you were in a good spot, a nice place. Okay, it was a priests' training college, and there wouldn't be motorbike displays, or the like. But it was a day out.

It was a day that changed my entire life.

The first memory I have of Drygrange, when we piled off the bus, was how wonderful the place smelled. Outside on that warm summer's day, in the middle of the soft Borders country, the air was filled with bees and birds and the smell of newly cut grass. We were met by a group of young men in their early twenties, dressed in jeans and tee-shirts, some with hair down to their shoulders, laughing and joking. The natural leader of the group introduced himself. 'Alright, folks. We're glad that you could make it. I hope you're ready to be hammered at football later.'

Eh? These weren't the sort of people I thought we'd be visiting. I expected robes, short-back-and-sides, Brylcream and black suits.

Memories of the rest of the visit remain imprinted on my mind like a yellowing creased photograph: faded, but still recognisable. As we crowded into the front hall, the first sight to greet us was a full-size snooker table! Not, as I might have imagined, a wall of holy paintings, or a display of priests' robes. A snooker table, and crowded round it, half-a-dozen or so students chatting, laughing, and smoking. There was an air of fun about the place, a sense of relaxed freedom. Where I had expected solemnity, I encountered familiarity, friendliness, and joy. Confused, my mind was in turmoil as I took in the scene.

The student who had greeted us spoke again. 'You're all very welcome here. I hope you enjoy your visit.'

That visit to Drygrange was when it all changed for me. Did Jesus enter my heart? Did the Holy Spirit plant a seed in my soul? Maybe. I'd never thought about the possibility of becoming a priest before the school visit. Undoubtedly it changed me fundamentally.

I was very quiet on the way home on the bus. All around me people were laughing and making fun: 'What a waste, them laddies goin' off to be priests.' But I remember so clearly that feeling of something changing, forever. Things falling into place. I there were questions too. Was the life of a priest one I could live? A life away from normal family living, yet so totally, unfathomably heroic.

A week later I was decided, and I announced to my mum that I thought I wanted to go to Drygrange to study to be a priest. She said she'd noticed my quietness ever since the visit; how withdrawn I'd become, how deep in thought I'd been. She was happy for her only child to be a priest, of that there was no doubt. Two weeks later, I was taken by my dad to see the parish priest in Dunfermline. From that moment on, at sixteen years of age, my path was set. The meeting itself was inconsequential; I was to help out on the altar, attend more Masses. I had found my way.

* * *

As I look back on it all now, it almost seems like an infatuation. It was irrational, deeply emotional. I was smitten. It's hard to explain now how I convinced myself that this was a pathway for me. I was never a pious child. I never dressed up as a priest or held mock Masses. I actually found the whole thing boring. But it's almost as though I accidentally tripped over on that visit to Drygrange and, as I fell, I clutched onto this notion that I could make everyone so proud of me by becoming a priest. And I would be happy, myself. In my experience very few priests have a flash-bang Damascene experience where the divinity speaks to them. More often it's a notion that grows organically and nags at you over time, an itch that never leaves you no matter how hard you scratch.

Irish Catholicism is steeped in centuries of mythology, and without a doubt that influenced me too. I had a great uncle, a priest in Ireland. He died having been wounded with shrapnel whilst saying Mass in Burma during the Second World War. Such stories helped to pull me deeper and deeper into the belief that God had chosen me. I believed with a certainty then, that I don't have now, that there was a God; that He particularly favoured Catholics and that He had chosen me to serve Him. My mother and father and I started then to kneel down every evening in my house before bed, to say the Rosary in order to nurture my vocation. The pressure was on.

I heard or read once that Irish mammies held a belief that having a son who was a priest was something akin to her getting a passport into heaven. All of these sociological and psychological forces undoubtedly would have impressed themselves on me. On the three of us. Combine this with a naïve anxiety, and desire to please others, and it is easy for me to understand that I believed I had a calling to be a priest from God Himself.

There was also something about those seminarians that I met on my visit. They were like me. They were – the ones I talked to anyway – working-class boys with long hair and humour. I made another few visits to Drygrange over the following couple of years, and learnt more about them. They smoked. They drank. They were kind and charismatic and good at football. I wanted to be their friend. I wanted to be like them. If these men could embrace such a life with humour and good grace, then so could I. I could, and I would, become a priest. I was certain of it.

2

TO THE BIG TREE AND BACK

St Andrew's College, Drygrange was, I was quick to learn, not a holy place.

This is surprising, given that it was the senior seminary for the east of Scotland, and was responsible for the training and development of many of Scotland's future priests, and some of its bishops too. As with much in life, my first impressions –formed on the school trip – were more of a romantic notion than a representation of the truth.

The building was a converted family home, a fairly grand one, which had seen various uses during the years. The staff at Drygrange were known as 'profs'. There were some who excelled in their academic field and were inspirational, but a significant number were uninspiring and, it seemed to me, cared little for the subjects they taught. The main faculty were all men, all priests.

Being a product of the Second Vatican Council (1962–65), the gathering of Church leaders and thinkers from across the globe who attempted to reassess how the Church related to the modern world, Drygrange was a seminary that was relaxed about the previous rules of dress and behaviour.

Priests and students rarely wore clerical garb except for high days and feast days. Previous rules about students always having to go out in groups of at least three (*numquam duo, semper tres,* 'never two, always three'), presumably to ward off the temptation of suspect or intimate relationships forming, were dismissed as passé. Students and staff routinely walked or drove into Melrose, where the pubs took the grant money from boys from the 'fairy castle', as Drygrange was known by some of the locals.

I always had the impression that being religiously orthodox in Drygrange gave students an extra barrier that they had to clamber over or slip under. The sense in the seminary was that it was right to push the notion of experimentation in how we practised religion. Overt piety, an over-indulgence in sanctity, always seemed to me to be regarded as suspicious, not just by the other students I mixed with but also by some of the priests who taught us. There was a hearty number of those more conservatively minded seminarians, though. Some of them were identified by the long black capes that they wore. They sat in the freezing chapel like ravens, and swished along the corridors as they went about their business.

The group I belonged to dressed in jeans, jumpers and trainers. I suppose we thought we looked like extras in an episode of *Starsky and Hutch.* But in reality, we probably looked like scruffs who thought our donkey-jackets gave us comradeship with the coal miners who were on strike at the time. We were the drinkers, the Irish rebel song-singers ('Come out, Ye Black and Tans/Come out and fight me like a man.'), the ones who sneered at the past, and saw our priesthood as being akin to guerrilla warfare.

Whatever 'group' you belonged to, it was a place busy with gossip and chatter, filled to the brim with men and people like me: not-yet-men who were working through their teenage fears and anxieties in an atmosphere that was not at all conducive to such a tremulous period of growth.

More than anything else, Drygrange had no clear leaders who made me want to say, 'Him. I want to be a priest just like him.' Except for one. The outstanding, charismatic figure, who embodied the priesthood with charm, wit, pleasantness and just that right hint of piety – the college spiritual director, Keith O'Brien.

K.O.B., as he was known, was an Irish charmer. His formative years in Scotland had not removed his soft lilting accent. Unlike most of the other profs, he routinely wore a black clerical shirt and trousers, but there was a wee quirk that made me take to him immediately. He opened the top button of his shirt and slid the white dog collar tab jauntily round so it was not on full show. Clerical casual.

We were introduced at morning coffee in the refectory where all staff and students met daily during weekdays. Not only did he look and sound different from the rest of the staff, his position also set him apart. As the college spiritual director, his role was no less than to lead you on your pathway to God, via the priesthood.

O'Brien also had one other important responsibility: he was, by mandate, the spiritual director and confessor of every first-year student in the college. After first year, we were free to approach another prof for spiritual direction, but, until then, O'Brien was our only choice. Routinely for one hour every fortnight, the new, usually young, seminarian would meet with him alone in his study. There the most intimate aspects of the student's spiritual journey would be discussed. O'Brien would hear our sins, and he would tell us they were forgiven through his ministry.

Drygrange celebrated its silver jubilee in 1977, a year prior to my entry through its doors. The college booklet outlining the role of the seminary included this key passage about the importance of the spiritual director:

> The primary purpose of a seminary is to train the young men who are to be our future Priests to be men of God, men of prayer. . . . No matter what intellectual training they receive, or how many examinations they pass, if they are not holy men, holy Priests, then they are failures –and the seminary has failed.
>
> Every encouragement and help is given to the seminarian as he develops in the life of prayer and tries to embrace the cross in his daily routine – with prudent guidance being given by the College Spiritual Director.

I felt then Keith – I was quickly on first-name terms with him – was a hugely benevolent presence in the college. In many cases, he was the antithesis of the other staff members. It was quite clear to me from the outset that he was ambivalent towards academic study. His main message was the power of prayer. He encouraged us young seminarians to accept that spending time praying, and in dialogue with God, was what would make us good priests. Holy priests. Like him.

* * *

I know a lot of things now that I didn't when I was eighteen and entering the seminary. I know now what an attraction the life of a priest has to homosexual men. I simply had never thought about it before I went there. Where I came from in Fife, being called a 'wee cunt' was a term of endearment. If someone called you a 'poof', though, that was trouble. If you put on aftershave that your aunt got you for Christmas and your pals caught your scent, then you were splashing on your 'poof juice', even though it had been advertised by the then British heavy-weight boxing champion.

So leaving my village and entering the seminary was a huge shock for me, because at Drygrange I encountered a blatant gay culture which involved a number of seminarians and profs. My teenage, unformed, mind was not prepared for this. When I saw big hairy men chase one another round the snooker table screaming with riotous laughter and eventually collapsing into a giggling heap as they tickled one another into spasms, I could not comprehend it. When I saw male couples walking arm in arm down to the 'big tree' halfway down the driveway and back, before or after lunch I was astounded. And when I observed some of the more flamboyant profs make eyes at some of the fresh young intakes and circle them like prowling tigers looking for prey, I felt deeply uneasy. Within a relatively short space of time my uneasiness at the gayness of Drygrange completely dissolved. But the sense of threat from one or two of the more predatory staff members, senior seminarians or visiting priests never left. There was, as we shall see, good reason for that caution.

The barely suppressed flamboyance of Drygrange did, on occasion, bubble over into an out-and-out gay picnic when fuelled by alcohol. Priestly culture in the east of Scotland in my day was a heavily drink-infused affair. It was accepted as the norm then. The staff frequently got plastered and the students followed their lead. Later, when we had been ordained and were in the parish as priests, many of us drank alone or with our priest pals.

Saints' feast days or special occasions in the Church year were excuses for 'bar nights' which invariably took place in the students' common room although, on more elevated occasions, the college Feast Day for St Andrew, for example, the staff common room was used. Once all the liturgy and ceremony were over, the drinking would begin. A sort of 'pop-up' pub was created, lights were dimmed into an intimate glow. Chairs and coffee tables were arranged into tight huddles. Seminarians, showered, talc-ed and shaved, meandered in wearing freshly ironed shirts. Faces shone, glancing about this transformed space looking for friends, intimates, fellow travellers.

It wasn't very long before even a näive vessel like me knew to watch for one particular prof who sought out one of the prettier students for a long and intense chat about . . . about what? I don't know, but I don't think it was about the mystery of the Holy Trinity.

Slowly, over months, I began to learn some of the secrets of Drygrange. I began to make some pals and, routinely in the evenings, groups of us would wander into and out of one another's rooms for a chat. I distinctly remember finding myself in one such situation, in what was the old

wing of the building, well away from my room in the pur-
pose-built new wing.

A group of us were lolling around in this older guy's
room. It was dark and gloomy and, to make it even more
atmospheric, this lad loved Leonard Cohen. With 'Sisters
of Mercy' playing in the background, we began discussing
the recent events that we'd heard about at a nearby church
where, apparently, the tabernacle with the Sacred Host – the
consecrated communion wafer that contained the 'real presence' of Jesus – was broken into and the contents stolen.
It never occurred to me that the solid gold chalices that
contained the Eucharist may be melted down and sold. We
agreed that the only reason for such a horrific thing to have
happened was … Satanism. The Eucharist must be being
sacrilegiously abused as we spoke. My spine shuddered in a
mixture of shock and fear. My heart beat faster. It was dark
outside now. Moonless. Leonard was now singing about his
stay in the Chelsea Hotel. Something about a head on an
unmade bed. The student whose room it was looked at us
solemnly. He was, he said, going to let us into a secret, but
we must promise not to breathe a word of it. We nodded.

The story concerned an incident that had happened the
year before we'd arrived. It occurred in the new wing. My
wing. My heart rate pulsed even faster. A seminarian had
died by suicide. We were told that the day after he had made
the attempt, when he was clinging onto life, the college
rector had called the entire community together to explain
the circumstances. He had asked them to pray like they had
never prayed before for the healing of their brother seminarian. And, they were cautioned, no-one was to speak of the

event to anyone. We were also told that this young man died a painful death.

If the story is true, and I have no reason to doubt it, this was my first encounter with the Church's default position in times of trouble: turn inward, stay silent, and act as if nothing occurred. No-one said anything. Not officially anyway. There could be no scandal. And, of course, no lessons could be learned.

The room was silent, except for the low moan of Leonard – 'Hey, that's no way to say goodbye'. How, in God's name, could such a thing have happened in a priests' training college? But I had something else on my mind. The room in the new wing, where the dead seminarian had slept, what number was it? He told us the number. It was my room. My pals glanced at me. There were some nervous chuckles but largely I just remember the silence, and eyes lowered to the floor. That night, I lay down on the bed that my recently dead predecessor had slept in, but sleep didn't find me.

* * *

My head was ablaze with it all – this new life. After a time, I found that I was not the only person who felt out of sorts and uncomfortable in those surroundings. Eventually I found students in the seminary with whom I was to get on well. They were generally people of a similar working-class, unsophisticated background. We agreed about the strangeness of Drygrange and the lifestyle. We agreed on our disgust at the food we were served, by the lack of heating in the chapel, by the strangeness of the profs and the difficulty of some of the topics we were to learn. This was a time where I had to take a dictionary to lectures and study sessions so that I could look up some of the terminology that our teachers threw at us. Hermeneutics, phenomenology, metaphysics, eschatology, apologetics – not words used in my life up till then.

The length of time for study in Drygrange to reach ordination was six years. The first two years were fundamentally philosophy-based. Then, for younger seminarians like me who had entered Drygrange straight from school or from the junior seminary at Blairs, near Aberdeen, you had to take a year out. The final four years was a more intensive course examining all aspects of theology. It was a challenging academic programme with exams twice a year. At the end of the course, students had to submit final papers in Scriptural Studies, Dogma and Moral Theology, and undergo intensive oral exams.

Many of the staff were not easy company. Aloof, aggressive, socially awkward. However, once I overcame my initial fear of them, I felt somewhat sorry for those men. I worked hard at trying to build relationships with each of them and once I did gain some sort of rapport I found that, despite their sometimes rude and abrupt manner, they weren't the complete horrors I'd previously dismissed them as being.

Imagining myself now in their position causes me to reflect on what a hard hand they'd been played. I can't say that I'd have survived any better than them if, after my ordination, I'd been ordered to become a staff member in Drygrange. Six or seven years of study and then maybe years of lecturing would, in all likelihood, have led me into the sort of institutionalisation that I was clearly observing in some of those men. It was as though they didn't understand Drygrange any more than I did, but they were sentenced to remain there for years. Maybe the bitterness, the social awkwardness, the snarking mannerisms and the drinking, were a consequence of hurt and disappointment due to the fact that they were lumbered with this unholy place, and we students were in turn lumbered with them.

As seminarians we could apply to the civil authorities and receive our full academic grants which went to the seminary and the remainder, once fees were accounted for, was handed back to us. All of that was fine. Except for one thing: Drygrange seminary offered no degree or qualification at the end of its six-year academic course. This was to be a major practical problem in later years when I was to apply for jobs after leaving the priesthood. It was also a significant ethically compromising stance for the Church to have taken. Although by the end of my training at Drygrange I was highly educated, I had no measurable officially recognised qualifications to show for it.

The fall-out rate was high. There were many reasons for that. In some cases, seminarians felt that their calling was simply not genuine, that God in fact did not want them to be a priest. Sometimes they simply changed their minds and decided they wanted to do something else. Another was an inability to keep up with the academic side of things. However, there was another reason that was always shrouded in mystery and fear to me, and many of my fellow seminarians. Twice a year the entire seminary faculty would begin the process of the *scrutinium*. At the end of the first and third term the staff would retreat into their common room and would discuss every single student, to judge their suitability to continue their studies towards the priesthood. This was a truly terrifying time. That shut door with the profs hidden away on the other side made me sick with anxiety. Not only was there the natural undergraduate worry of exams and whether or not you'd passed them, there was the added worry of whether, at some point over the past few months, you might have inadvertently offended one of the profs and it would come up at the 'scrutes', as they were called. Thinking about it now, that very system of unaccountable power over students' lives, and the abuse that flows from it, is a microcosm of the power imbalance that lies at the heart of so many of the problems felt in Catholicism today.

On the last day of term, all the students gathered at the snooker table where envelopes containing their exam results were laid out, and then we were called in individually for a meeting with the rector. That was the time when you heard whether or not you had made it through. Many did not. At the end of my first term many students were culled for some infringement or other. There was never any appeal, because no such process existed.

In amongst the fear and anxiety of worry about academic life and the travails of living in such a strange community, I found spiritual direction from Keith O'Brien to be a welcome relief. Very quickly, Keith's charm worked on me. As I've indicated, he was the most 'priestly' priest of the whole faculty. Simply put, he was at ease in talking about Jesus. Other profs did in their lectures and, of course, at Mass and services, but maybe because of his role as spiritual director Keith had a more intimate contact that convinced me at the time that he truly was a holy man. He also had a keen sense of humour and fun: he could be scathing of others as the trust between us grew and he was able to share some gossip. In many ways he was my antidote to the rest of college life.

Keith and I also had a few things in common. As an ordained priest he had taught in St Columba's RC High School – the same school I had attended – albeit before my time. However, we both knew some of the staff there. He was closely connected with one Fife family that I also was friendly with. All of this gave us an easy familiarity from the off.

He often described the role of the priest as being a man of prayer, and that, being in prayer, communing with Christ, was our reason for being. He gave me no doubts at all that I would one day be elevated to the brotherhood of the priesthood, but I must pray and then pray more. This was the first time I'd heard the priesthood described as a 'brotherhood'. I remember him talking about the intense pleasure it was to confess his sins to our shared friend who had just recently been ordained a priest. He looked forward to doing the same to me in a few years. As time passed, I was to understand more of what that actually might mean.

As weeks of spiritual direction passed, what had started as an easy familiarity grew into an even closer friendship. I observed that Keith, like almost every other member of staff, recruited a close group of favoured students around him. This was the in-crowd he'd laugh with the most, the ones he'd whisper to while passing in the corridor. Being invited by Keith into Melrose for a bar supper was a sought-after prize. I became a member of that close court that Keith created around himself. It was fun, it was comfortable. Keith would give you the nod earlier in the day: 'Meet me at the back door and we'll go to Melrose for a bite to eat later.' Exclusive. Close. Brotherly. I remember sitting next to him when a small group of us went to see "One Flew Over The Cuckoo's Nest" in the nearby town, Keith whispering which students and profs the patients were like. Us all giggling. At that time, completely in the dark.

In 1979, at the end of September, Pope John Paul II visited Ireland. Keith announced that he and another priest intended going over and joining in the celebrations with a coach party. An offer was made to take a group of seminarians who wanted to join the trip. I was quick to volunteer. To see the Pope, and to get that intense and connected time with Keith himself away from the college, was something that I simply could not miss. We set out on the long, tiring journey fuelled by the excitement of it all.

It's my first real memory of the status that being a student priest gave me amongst Catholics beyond the walls of Drygrange. The other people on the coach must have observed our familiarity with our spiritual director; the laughs we shared, our in-jokes and the informal closeness. But there was also an intimacy, an exclusivity, within our small Drygrange group. Keith was not participating in the papal Masses himself, but he still had an obligation to say Mass daily, so we seminarians met in his bedroom every morning. His coffee table was made into a makeshift altar where he said Mass with our little group. It felt like being initiated into some sort of exclusive spiritual cult.

I didn't know it then of course, I didn't have the words, but I was being groomed by him, and I'm sure that if I had lost his confidence my days in Drygrange would have been numbered. His patronage was all that was required for a student's stupidity – and in my case participation in a cruel act towards one of the college helpers – to be overlooked. He had that power. We both knew it. The incident I participated in still haunts me.

A few men from a nearby institution for people with learning disabilities used to work part time in Drygrange doing odd jobs. One of them always used to make an appearance in the refectory at lunchtime on his birthday. He'd make a short speech and then blow out the candles on his cake, which the college supplied to applause and singing from students and faculty. It would have been one of the highlights of his year. On this occasion Keith had bought some candles that reignited after they were blown out. He thought it would be funny to see how the man reacted. He asked me to light the candles and carry the cake out. Like a puppy ever eager to please, I did so. When the man blew out the candles and they immediately relit, the expression on his face was one of sheer incomprehension. He blew again. Again the candles re-ignited. The refectory was a cacophony of riotous laughter. Faces thrown back and red. But it was no joke. We were making a fool of this man; we were laughing at his distress from a perspective of smug superiority. It was grotesque.

Not everyone was laughing though. When I returned to my seat, some of the staff members were furious with me. They knew, despite all their perceived flaws, what I'm ashamed to say I didn't –that a great cruelty had occurred. My defence? Keith had told me to do it.

Spiritual direction sessions with Keith invariably consisted of him asking how I was getting on at the college; how I was doing with the studies and what difficulties I had in adapting to life in the seminary. He always heard my confession at the end of the session.

Remembering the anonymity of confession prior to entering the seminary – the dark box, the kneeler, the grille, the faceless voice – the much more informal confession which happened face to face during spiritual direction had a huge effect on me. It took a long time to adjust to, as Keith's presence, his nearness, his eye contact, magnified his physical proximity. I grew to like it, as I felt I was able to unburden myself to my friend. At the end of confession Keith would lay both of his hands on my head and say the words of absolution. I remember he used to add in something like 'Son, I absolve you from the sins that you've confessed and all the other sins you may have committed in your life.' This was handy, given my anxiety over having perhaps missed some sin or other in my past. Even the forgotten ones were forgiven.

Then there was Keith's embrace. Men hug. Even in my emotionally stunted youth I hugged men or my pals as we played or were happy or sad. My dad always kissed me openly and I kissed him when we met or parted. Keith had taken to calling himself my spiritual father, but his embrace at the end of the spiritual direction session was different from anything shared with my own father. It was longer and with more intimacy. It had a physicality to it that was not just a recognition of affection. He had a curious manner of brushing my cheek with his own. I could feel his bristly skin. I don't remember being concerned about it or feeling endangered by it at first. I put it down to the fact that Keith, this paragon priest, really liked me. However, as time passed he would take to putting his hand under the back of my shirt during our embraces. I remember the shock of his cold hand on my naked back. It was the first time anyone had touched my back since my mum bathed me as a child, or a nurse clothed me on the ward at the Sick Children's Hospital in Edinburgh. I did feel uncomfortable about that. What could I do though? Who could I talk to about it? Where could I seek guidance when it was my own spiritual guide whose hands were wandering?

Well, in my case, I couldn't seek it anywhere.

I felt helpless, really. The embarrassment and shock of it. And the loneliness of not being able to discuss it with anyone who might challenge him, because to do so would spell the end of my time in Drygrange. I had no doubt about that. It was just something I reconciled myself to. I did hear a story about another seminarian getting very upset about Keith's hug at the end of his spiritual direction session. The rumour spread quickly and then stopped. That student didn't make it through his course. In fact, he left fairly soon after I heard the story.

* * *

That first Christmas holiday in 1978 was my first extended period at home after starting at Drygrange. Traumatised by the culling in the *scrutinium* of so many students whom I'd begun to know, and by the exams that I'd, fortunately, passed, I was glad to be with my mum and dad and sleeping again in my own bed. I remember my mum saying that I'd changed during that first term – I now drank whisky which I'd never done before. I had even bought a pipe. I was eighteen and smoking a pipe.

Was she seeing the 'trappings' of the priestly lifestyle? I never gave it too much thought at the time. I do believe that what I was trying to do was to put a brave and grown-up face on. I was enjoying being a seminarian despite the breath-taking strangeness of Drygrange. It gave me status, and fuelled a sense of self-worth, and that heroism I originally associated with the school visit a few years before (Not that anyone else thought I was heroic: I chose to put myself as the main character in my own fantasy).

As the seasons and the terms passed, I began to appreciate more and more how spectacularly beautiful the Borders of Scotland is. When the winter snow eventually thawed out and the daffodils began to bloom, life at Drygrange seemed so much easier to cope with. Daffodils still have a special place in my heart.

As my worries and anxieties about the gay culture of Drygrange dissipated, I made friends with a lot of gay men in the seminary. One of them even came out to me once, which was a source of personal pride (Although when I spoke to him about it a few weeks later he'd changed his mind and popped back into his closet again).

Brideshead Revisited was playing as a TV series at the time, and the common room where it was shown was as busy as it might have been for Scotsport; just a different crowd. I even agreed to participate in the annual play that we put on for the old ladies and gents of the surrounding area as well as invited families and friends. The production was *See How They Run* by Philip King. I played the part of the Reverend Lionel Toop. Of course, all of the parts, male and female, were played by us seminarians. We took on our roles with more vigour than talent perhaps. But embrace them we did. And that embrace taught me a lot about life and acceptance, diversity and awareness. Later on, I was to become an activist in the AIDS field after leaving the priesthood. A straight man in a gay world was my normal for many, many years. For that, Drygrange prepared me well and I owe it a lot. I still laugh when I remember being told about a conversation that took place in my final year between two seminarians who were junior to me. They had been going through the student list, trying to work out who was gay and who wasn't. I was told that when they came to me they said "Brian isn't gay. He just wishes he was."

There was a lot of sport in Drygrange. Mostly football, even though the Borders' dominant game is rugby. Some of the boys were outstanding footballers, particularly – it seemed to me – those from the west of Scotland, Motherwell and the surrounding areas. There were a few who could have taken the sport up at a more senior level, I'm sure. They definitely made us a tricky team to play against in the local leagues that we joined.

I was an average player, a left back, but I was strong enough (some might say a 'dirty player') and was quite happy to put in some harsh tackles on our opponents. I was routinely picked for the side. I remember though one day the captain announced that I was to be a substitute, and another student would take my place. I was aghast. A group of young people were visiting the college at the time and some were watching the match. This was supposed to be my time to show off in front of them. As the first half got underway I couldn't really see that the guy who replaced me was any great shakes, so I got a couple of the girl spectators to shout out 'Get Brian Devlin on!' frequently before half time. They made quite a racket now I think of it. Come half-time and the halved oranges, the captain sidled up to me. 'Right, you've made your point. You're on!' I raised a thumb to my little group of fans who waved back all smiles, happy with our collaboration.

At Drygrange I also discovered jogging. I wasn't much of a runner, but there was a long period when I'd head off on a run for a few miles. I loved the sense of freedom and accomplishment it gave me. I suppose there was an element of fulfilment in arriving back at the front door sweating and panting, before a quick shower and down to morning prayer.

Of course the chapel was where a great part of the day was spent. It was a modern addition to the grounds of the house. Not for us any of the lavish baroque gilding that many churches display. Ours was bare, modern, uncluttered, and functional. At one end to the right of the entrance door was the sacristy, where the priests vested before Mass. In the chapel itself seminarians sat in choir stalls on either side in monastic style, and at the opposite end to the sacristy, on a slightly raised platform, was the simple wooden altar. On either side of that were the stalls where the priests sat.

Our liturgies were often 'experimental' for the day. At one point in the Mass, after the sermon and once the bread and wine had been received from whatever seminarians were chalked up to carry it to the officiating priest, all of the students would rise and stand in a semi-circle around the altar as the Eucharistic Prayer was read. This is the part of the Mass where the priest utters the words that change the Communion wafer and the altar wine into the actual body and blood of Jesus. The theological term for this is 'transubstantiation'. For Catholics this is the central point of their belief: that Jesus' real presence is there in the now-consecrated bread and wine. I used to find this, especially in my first year, very moving. It was as though I was an active part of the ritual rather than just an observer. The more liturgically conservative seminarians tutted at this practice, but I enjoyed it.

Another new thing for me was that Communion was delivered through both the wafer and also from the chalice containing what was now, we believed, Christ's blood. Once again, these liturgical innovations, now widely practised throughout the Catholic world, were progressive and inclusive.

I do remember even these innovations attracted gossip. Those were the early days of AIDS, and news of the 'gay plague' was filtering through to us. What wasn't filtering through so clearly was how you could, and couldn't, 'catch' it. I remember one of my pals whispering his worries to me that he was going to refuse to sip from the Communion chalice in case he caught AIDS from the saliva of one of our gay comrades who had supped ahead of him.

We also had regular group Masses. The student body was split into a number of groups made up of both junior and senior members of the seminary. This structure was designed to offer a support network, and many members did bond well together and went out for meals and so on. But the group Mass was the focal point. The lad whose turn it was to arrange proceedings, would approach one of the profs to say the Mass, and arrange his room into a little chapel for the event. Chalices and candles were borrowed from the sacristy and music was chosen.

I vividly remember one group Mass that was arranged in a dark, cold outbuilding attached to the main house. We were to sit on whatever was available on the dirty floor. All we had was candlelight to see by. The theme of the Mass was poverty and how we were called to serve the poor and the helpless. It was lovely, and earnest. But I was so happy when it was over and I could get stuck into the pasta bolognese that was on the menu.

* * *

At the start of every academic year, a list was put up on the notice board of specially allocated jobs. I'd mentioned in my admission interview that I had worked in a holiday job in the gardens of various Dunfermline hospitals. I must have appeared more enthusiastic about the work than I actually was, because I was made assistant gardener in my first year. I was good at following orders but didn't really know one end of a flower from another in those days.

However, as I became more senior I was lucky enough to be given the job of sacristan. Basically, this involved ensuring that the chapel and the priests' vestments were all in order for the coming week. This was a great wee gig. On the afternoons dedicated to manual work, while the rest were out on the farm or trimming the rhododendrons, I had the chapel to myself. Out came the floor polisher with which I would polish that wooden floor until it shone. It was a slippery enough surface at the best of times, so the knack was to apply just the right amount of liquid polish so that it looked pristine, but was not too deadly underfoot.

The chapel was mine for that period. As the sun streamed in or the rain beat down, I was happy in my world. Occasionally another student would be dispatched to help me. My feeling about that was inevitably mild irritation. I'd rather have been on my own, but I gave him his tasks and made sure he knew what he had to do. I was a benevolent dictator in those days, in *my* chapel.

Whilst it was to be a source of the greatest pleasure in those days of manual work, the chapel was also where I experienced my most profound discomfort.

I did not know how to pray.

I could say by rote the usual Our Fathers and Hail Marys of course, but I didn't get the feeling in any sense that this was what Keith O'Brien meant when he was telling me to commune with the Lord. I was distracted by anything and everything. When I observed other students and members of staff in the chapel, deep in prayer and serene in contemplation, I panicked. My brain jumped from topic to topic.

'Oh, Lord, come to my aid. Oh, Lord, make haste to help me. In the name of the Father and of the Son and the Holy Spirit - Old Chris has got a stain down the front of his crotch again - Mary, Mother of God, pray for – it's freezing in here – us. St Joseph – where's that smell of eggs coming from? – pray for us. Cry out with joy –who's Joy? – to the Lord, all the earth – I'm so bored – and serve the Lord with gladness.

Know that he, the Lord, is God. – Jesus-loves-me-I-know-fine – He made us, – because-I-gave-Him-ten-Woodbine – we belong to Him, –I-smoked-one-and-He -smoked-nine –we are his people, the sheep of his flock – Jesus-loves-me-I-know-fine. Amen.'

I was in a fast-spin cycle with diversions tumbling around, wanting to be anywhere but where I was. I'm pretty sure I wasn't alone in all this, but I could have been stuck on top of Mount Everest, such was my sense of being out of place. A priest who is unable to pray, it seemed to me at the time, is like being a blind surgeon or a mute opera singer. I felt wretched, isolated and embarrassed. I wanted to listen and to hear what God was saying to me but couldn't. There was too much background noise.

We had frequent spiritual retreats at Drygrange during term time, some of them held in silence. Visiting priests would engage us in various spiritual exercises: Ignation Spirituality or Contemplative Prayer and so on. During this time we were to give ourselves over entirely to the meditative practices that we were being taught. There would be time for us to meet the retreat master individually to discuss any issues we were having, and I availed myself of those occasions. The truth is, I was, especially in the first few years, like a puppy. I'd bound up to a new idea of what prayer might mean, shake it about a bit and then become bored with it and cast it aside with the other chewed-up toys. I discussed all of this with O'Brien who told me to get close to Jesus, that a priest had to be a man of prayer.

Then the big change came along, that was to change the nature of prayer so fundamentally that the background tinnitus almost disappeared. Maybe more accurately the background din became the prayer itself. Originating from Pentecostalism, the Charismatic Renewal Movement spread like a fire throughout the Roman Catholic Church in Scotland and beyond during the 1970s and '80s. It celebrated the feast of Pentecost, when the Holy Spirit was said to descend on Christ's followers, and they began to sing praise to the Lord and spoke in strange and unknown languages. This was colloquially known as 'speaking in tongues'.

The music attached to the movement was vibrant, upbeat and joyful, and as far away as you could get from the morose dirges sung in most churches across Scotland. In Drygrange the Charismatic Renewal Movement moved in, took up lodgings, and was either loved or reviled depending on which side of the fence you sat. Keith O'Brien championed this type of prayer and celebration. By its nature it was happy and – literally – clappy. There was a lot of hand holding, of embracing, of 'praying over' each other, and for those premier division pray-ers, there was praying in tongues.

O'Brien used to take a small group of us, his insiders, up to Edinburgh in his car to attend Charismatic Renewal days in Craiglockhart College every month or so. Craiglockhart was then the Roman Catholic teachers' training college. These Saturdays became a necessary fix for me. Not only did I love Charismatic Renewal, the college was a great place to be in the company of women. In normal parish Masses, when the priest says: 'Let us offer one another the sign of peace', it is usually an embarrassed handshake to those around you, with eyes averted. But in a Charismatic Mass there were many embraces and kisses. All very chaste, but it was the high spot of my month. To smell the perfume and feel the soft, scented skin of the women students more than made up for the two-hour round trip.

The prayer was loud; eyes were shut or raised to the ceiling, arms were open as if waiting to catch an infant falling from a blazing first-floor window. People swayed and smiled. Softly they prayed:

'Oh praise you, Jesus. Praise you my dear, Lord. We welcome your Spirit, Lord, Praise you, praise our Father, we love you, Lord Jesus. PRAISE YOU, LORD.' Then the tone would rise. On a signal from the leader of these praise sessions, guitars would set a tone from the 'music ministry'. The prayer would intensify 'WE PRAISE JESUS. WE WELCOME YOU, LORD. YOU ARE THE HOLY ONE, LORD. YOU ARE THE LORD. SEND YOUR SPIRIT, LORD.'

And first softly and then growing in a crescendo: '*Oo Shalalachem. Kryosimum marananacheem.*'

All around the packed hall people singing in tongues, each in their own reverie invoking the presence of the Holy Spirit. Was it really a manifestation of God or was it some form of hysterical group reaction? I don't know. I do, however, know that it was very moving and intense. Personally, I was never any good at the 'tongues' thing. I did try but sounded like I was chanting for rain. I guess I didn't have the gift. The 'charism' as it's called. I was just a Fife laddie who didn't know what he was doing really. I stuck to plain old English chanting: 'Praise you, Jesus. I'm a potato, Lord. Peel me. I'm a can of Coke, Lord. Make me fizz with your spirit.'

3

NIGHT PRAYER

The Charismatic Movement eventually became, as such movements eventually do, less appealing as time ticked on. Its literalism to the Word of Scripture opened the door for all kinds of prejudice to take root. However, for people like me at that time, people who couldn't pray, but only recite, people who couldn't commune, only babble, it was God-sent. Keith O'Brien thought so too.

If O'Brien needed an excuse for close physical contact, then being 'charismatic' in all senses of that word gave him one. Our spiritual direction sessions would typically include him sitting on a footstool in front of his electric fire, clasping both of my hands in his and praising the Lord: '*Ooo calanachim, spiriam achamer seeolius*'. He, clearly, did have the charism.

By then O'Brien was taking greater and greater risks physically with me. With his embraces he was teaching me that these outward signs of affection were nothing more than that. Just two close friends being, well, 'charismatically friendly'.

Frequently he would pick me and a pal up in Edinburgh on a Saturday night late on and drive us back to Drygrange after we had had a day off, been with our families and then met in the city to visit the pubs. My pal always got in the back seat of the car and fell asleep. I always got in the front seat. In the dark of the journey O'Brien would place his hand on my arm and start to rub it. He would hold my hand. He would stroke my thigh. I never responded in any way at all.

Like his embrace and the shock of his cold hand on my back under my shirt, I didn't understand what was going on. I didn't understand sex or grooming. I would likely have been slightly drunk when it happened. And the strange thing is we never discussed it. I don't remember ever having a serious discussion with him about the unease I felt with the behaviour of some of the seminarians and staff in Drygrange, but I do have a recollection of him once speaking to the student body about the need for us all to conduct ourselves as 'manly men'. This stuck in my mind because a few of us used the term 'manly men' as an almost satirical trope to show that we were certainly not part of the openly gay crowd. 'Manly men doing manly things' was how we described ourselves. In effect what we were really being told was that appearances are important. Behaviour is one thing, but two other realities are more significant. Get caught out behaving inappropriately and you're on your own. You will be asked to close the door behind you as you depart. Secondly, don't attract attention to yourself. Being 'manly men' was not an appeal for us to search for our true authentic male nature. It was a warning against the kind of behaviour which might attract unwelcome attention, and questioning, from outside.

I was naïve about sex. In fact, truth be told, I think one of the attractions of the seminary for me was the thought of the avoidance of sex all together, with its sinful consequences.

But, as I've said, I was highly tuned into the reality of the power O'Brien had over me. I knew that if I displeased or challenged him I would be a casualty at the next *scrutinium*.

Eventually this increasing tension had to spill over.

It never, not for an instant, struck me as odd that a man twenty years my senior would invite me into his bedroom to say Compline, or night prayers, with him because that man was my friend, my hero, and my idol.

At the end of many of the days it became almost a domestic routine. Keith would knock on my door (I'd moved to the old wing by then) or pass me in the corridor and suggest we share the last part of the Divine Office, the cycle of prayers that all priests are supposed to structure their day around. One Friday night towards the end of my second year, as I was preparing for my year away from the seminary, was just such an occasion. Keith was always left a vacuum flask of warm malted milk drink by the nuns in the seminary. He would pick it up on the way to his bedroom at the end of the day. This particular evening the staff had had their evening meal together. They were generally boozy affairs. I could see he'd been drinking, but he was not falling-over drunk.

When he called me to join him in his bedroom I was, as always, pleased to see him. As usual, we both sat down. The room was sparsely furnished and functional. The single bed was made up and tidy. I never really liked the taste of malted milk, but as he poured it out of the little red tartan flask into two cups, I enjoyed the warmth of the liquid through the cup.

As usual, the liturgy began. He started, 'O Lord, come to my aid,' and I responded, 'O Lord, make haste to help us.'

He continued: 'Glory be to the Father, the Son and the Holy Spirit. As it was in the beginning, is now and ever shall be, world without end. Amen.'

We paused for a period of silent reflection on the failings and the sins we had committed during the day. We called on Mary, the Virgin, to help us. Together we murmured our prayer:

> Hail, holy Queen, Mother of mercy,
> hail, our life, our sweetness and our hope.
> To thee do we cry, poor banished children of Eve:
> to thee do we send up our sighs,
> mourning and weeping in this vale of tears.
> Turn then, most gracious Advocate,
> thine eyes of mercy toward us,
> and after this our exile, show unto us the blessed
> fruit of thy womb, Jesus,
> O merciful, O loving, O sweet Virgin Mary! Amen.

And finally:

> Save us, Lord, while we are awake; protect us while
> we sleep; that we may keep watch with Christ and
> rest with him in peace.
> The Lord grant us a quiet night and a perfect end.
> Amen.

We laid our cups, empty now, on the table as our prayer concluded with him blessing me. Placing his hands on the top of my head he said, 'Son, I bless you in the name of the Father, the Son and the Holy Spirit. Amen.'

At the end of the evening Keith would usually envelop me in his hug and then I would leave. However, on that night something different happened. He did hug me . . . but it was for far longer than it had ever been before, with a greater intensity. I remember as I turned to leave, he sat down and pulled me on top of him. My first reaction was of total confusion. Had he stumbled because of the drink and pulled me down accidentally? But then he put his arms around me. I felt a fleeting sense of how ridiculous this was: nearly six-foot-tall me sitting on this much older man's knee. He began to caress me. He told me that he loved me. At that point I was asking myself if he was joking. But then it became clear that he wasn't. He told me that he would always love me. With ever more urgency he rubbed my arms and chest. My embarrassment turned to shame and to fear.

What was he doing? Why was he behaving like this? This isn't how it should be. I saw my idol, the holiest man I had ever known, disintegrate in front of me.

My dad frequently and tenderly told me that he loved me. Here was Keith O'Brien, the priest who'd taken to calling himself my spiritual father, saying the same words. But it was clear they meant something different and were demanding a response that was not in my mental vocabulary to give.

Did he register the shock, the confusion and the vulnerability in my eyes? I had smiled in my friend's presence so many times. Did he somehow think this had been a sign of anything other than sincere friendship? What did he think when he looked at me in his bedroom?

No-one in my life up until that point had declared their love for me in the way that O'Brien had done – with such intensity and with such passion. When he said, 'I love you; I have a secret, a big secret that I'm not able to share with you just yet. But I will never stop loving you, come what may', he was telling me something that had never crossed my mind before: he wanted me to be bound to him. Up until that very point, I had needed him. But now he was telling me that *he* needed *me*.

I stood up and gently but firmly pulled away from his grasp, saying 'Goodnight, Keith.' He was silent. He didn't pursue me or call out to me as I made for the door. He must have known that he had made a terrible miscalculation. I, for my part, was in full flight mode. I had spent a lot of my two years in this man's presence. Now I was scared and confused, and wanted to get as far away from him as possible.

I closed the door to his bedroom quietly and walked the few steps to my own room, with a burning sense of shame, more shaken than I had never felt before. My heart was thumping in my chest as I closed the door and got ready for bed.

What had I done? I asked myself. Had I unknowingly led my friend down this path? Of course, it must all be my fault. That's the automatic response that many people feel when they are the subject of deeply unwanted sexual advances. I must have led him into thinking that his feelings would be reciprocated, that somehow we could have some sort of romantic relationship.

It was not the quiet night, nor the perfect end I had prayed for.

Finally, I fell into an uneasy and brief sleep. When I woke up Keith was standing next to my bed. There was nothing particularly unusual in that, as without my hearing aid in, I could not hear the alarm clock. I frequently got a neighbour to wake me, especially for an early morning start.

As I fumbled about for my hearing aid, O'Brien waited. He looked gaunt and grey. It wasn't just a hangover he was suffering from. He leaned over me, and I flinched and tightened. For God's sake, I thought. Was he going to start on me again? But no. He said in a low voice that he meant every word of what he had said and apologised about his behaviour. He hoped I could forgive him.

I told him everything was fine (I was too shocked and confused to say otherwise). I told him I forgave him. What else could I do?

On reflection, what O'Brien was doing was confessing. Not to God, but to me. Everything about him was about risk – the touching in the car, the embracing, the hand under my shirt, and now this occurrence at night prayer. He took risks continuously. They were largely deniable risks – 'his-word-against-mine' risks. They were often taken under the cover of copious amounts of alcohol. Without doubt, his confession and plea for forgiveness was a way of preventing me from talking about it further. Although I wasn't bound by any real seal of confession, he did morally bind me into silence that morning.

Was this 'morning after' pill, though, something that he used to even greater effect with ordained priests when he was their archbishop? I believe it very well might have been. And if true then it carries a heavy canonical penalty and it results in one of the Church's most devastating punishments. It's called excommunication, '*latae sententiae*', and I will explore it in detail in the second part of this book.

That Saturday morning after O'Brien woke me, I went down to prayer and sat on my customary bench, which happened to be almost directly opposite where he and the other priests sat during prayers and Mass. I looked at him as he sat solemnly, fighting what might have been a tough hangover, demure in the moment, and at that instant I gained an important, life-changing insight. I felt with certainty that O'Brien was a conman and a sham. His communing was entirely cynical. We were to find out many years into the future quite how deeply that cynicism went.

And the secret that he said he couldn't divulge to me as he told me of his love for me? It was that he had been asked by Cardinal Gray, the Church's most senior cleric in Scotland, to become rector of the junior seminary at Blair's, Aberdeen. The place where young boys who believed that God was calling them to the priesthood were sent at the age of twelve through to eighteen.

But Keith O'Brien's time at Drygrange was over. I had to get on with my studies and preparation for the priesthood, secure, at that time, in the belief that he would hold no authority over me again.

4

GOLD IS TESTED IN FIRE

After my second year, I had a compulsory gap year away from Drygrange. It was really a year to 'test' your vocation I think. Also, to earn a bit of money. But me being me, I spent it in a monastery with a religious group called the *Focolare* in Frascati, near Rome. It was a strange experience. It was a sort of commune of priests and seminarians from across the world involving the '*comunione dei beni*' (communion of goods), which meant that there was no individual ownership of anything, and everything was shared. I used to pass a *gelateria* nearly every day. I'd look in the window, awestruck by the range and flavours of ice cream. But since I never had any money, I was never able to enter. Many years later I took my wife to see the place. At the *gelateria* I made sure we both had the most indulgent ice creams we could afford, in order to cancel out some of those missed opportunities from the past.

When I returned home in the summer, I learned that a close friend of mine in the seminary had terminal cancer. That, and the constant unease I felt following the episode with O'Brien in Drygrange, led to the first time that I experienced the deep and insistent pull of depression. I actually went to the local GP about it. He told me a change of study would be the best for my health.

I wondered if I had the necessary internal resources to go back into my third year and the start of my theology course. But I was caught in a terrible quandary. My family's expectation that I would get ordained was unshakeable. To fail in that would be unspeakably awful. Yet I was experiencing a deeply unsettling feeling about whether or not I was on the right path. What's more, there was a growing fear the fear that perhaps what had happened to me at the hands of O'Brien was just an example of what went on in parish houses across the country.

So what were my options? To leave and deeply upset my family? Or to stay in the seminary and stick it out and put the whole O'Brien situation down to experience? At the end of the summer, my fear of leaving outweighed my fear of staying. That may have been a cowardly choice on my part. But it was the one I made.

When I returned to Drygrange I became more and more engrossed with the academic aspect of life there. I was a hard worker: not naturally as gifted as others were who seemed to sail through exams with the minimum of study. Dogged, determined, 'in it for the long term' was my approach.

I vividly remember opening up a large blank writing pad, bought before the start of term in a stationery store in Dunfermline, and flicking through the empty pages until I got to around three quarters in and writing 'You're still here'. A message to myself from myself. The worry that I'd get kicked out for some infringement or other was all pervasive. It was a small boost to remind myself that had not happened, when I feared it might. That worry also lead me to work even harder, which in turn earned me some fairly good pass marks.

I also managed my return by adopting a sort of fatalistic 'rope-a-dope' philosophy as term after term passed. Much as my sporting hero Muhammad Ali took a thrashing in the boxing ring until George Foreman tired himself out, I adopted a passivity, an outwardly eager but internally shut-down persona. Any true spiritual light inside me had been extinguished. I adopted a more academic and intellectual-ised approach to priesthood. I ploughed all of my effort into understanding and appreciating the beauty of theology and its revelations on the mystery of existence.

It's hard for me to judge now whether I was much of a role-model for junior students. I tried to be. But that's for others to decide. I suspect I was not as encouraging as I should have been.

Entry into the priesthood is a phased process. There are various minor or lay ministries such as lector and acolyte that the student goes through first. While relatively trivial in and of themselves, they were, like my scribbled note in the writing pad, markers of the journey: milestones along the path towards the major orders of diaconate in the fifth year, and, around twelve months later, priesthood itself.

Once I adopted my coping strategy, I found a degree of con-tentment in Drygrange. Certainly, the setting in the Borders countryside helped greatly. It was a place of great humour at times. Practical jokes were made and played. Nonsense, bor-dering on anarchy, always seemed to bubble away under the surface. Like my home village in Fife, any hint of grandeur or pomposity was a balloon that was quickly pricked.

I remember on one solemn occasion an important Mass was being said by Cardinal Gray in the chapel. The students were formally dressed in black cassocks and white surplices. Those serving the Mass were queued up waiting to proceed to the altar, close to the choir stalls where the rest of the student body stood. One lad was carrying a processional candle fixed into a large brass, highly polished, candlestick. He was waiting for the procession to move forward when one of my pals leaned over from the choir stall and swiftly and nonchalantly blew the candle out. Such was the tension of the event that that single, silly act caused the entire student body to collapse in fits of laughter. The poor boy holding his now useless candle had a look of total alarm on his face. Gamely, as I remember, he carried on his way as though his candle was glowing brightly.

I was so attracted to that rebelliousness within Drygrange – that constant shake-up of authority and structure. Small acts of defiance, in the face of what we thought were nonsensical rules, appeared like glorious victories. I suppose, in reality, we were just annoyances for the profs; immature adolescents, really, who thought we were going to change the Church by bursting a few of its bubbles.

Looking back now, I think I grew into Drygrange the more I grew into young adulthood. I came to love theology, and the more I learned about it, the more I relaxed into the place. My initial alarm over the gay culture of the seminary dissipated. It was just a fact of life. Actually, the only subject that, over my seven years of formation, I really excelled in was in the sphere of ethics, and particularly the realms of sexual and medical ethics. My final exam, based on my submitted paper, was a critique of the Church's ethical teaching on homosexuality.

Now that O'Brien was no longer at Drygrange, I found more honourable spiritual guides to lead me on what was still to be a rocky path to the priesthood. By the end of my third year, I experienced a total loss of faith in God, in the Church, in any of the supernatural presences that I was being taught about and reading about in my studies. It was as though the words of the prophet Isaiah, had taken root within me: 'Truly, you are a God who conceals Himself, God of Israel, Saviour (45:15).' God, the presence, the feeling, and the understanding lay deeply hidden from me. Such a profound loss of faith is not an unusual occurrence in the religious life. Mystics and teachers refer to it as a 'dark night of the soul', a term coined by St John of the Cross.

It's hard to describe what I felt in a comprehensible way. The loss of faith in structures and concepts was one part of it. But the other, more pervasive, sense was one of being hollowed out, of being unable to see or hear or taste or feel anything of God. It was sheer emptiness. Except for once.

I was reflecting on the phrase 'God loves you' in the chapel and I just kept repeating it again and again to myself silently: 'God loves you, God loves you, God loves you.' The normal babble in my brain ceased for a while as the words, and their meaning, sank into me. There was no heavenly choir. Just a feeling of peaceful contentment. It probably lasted a few seconds. Then it disappeared. Its memory though, is a rich one. It remains with me to this day. It was as though a door had opened for a fleeting instant and light had flooded in. Then, just as quickly, it clicked shut and a lock was turned. Maybe the fact that I did experience something beyond the locked door was enough to keep me fighting in the ring until my ordination?

Preparation for the priesthood, as I have already noted, takes a seminarian through several different stages towards ministry. Second only to ordination to the priesthood is that of becoming a deacon. At that point you become a fully paid-up member of the 'brotherhood'. You buy a new black suit and a new pair of shoes. You wear a priest's clerical shirt and collar and, to all intents and purposes, do almost everything a priest does. This is also the time that the seminarian makes the 'big' promises: to be obedient to his bishop and his successors is one. To live a celibate life is another.

At that stage, it was celibacy that was most on my mind. Recently I came across a reflection I wrote on my future vow before I became ordained. Five weeks before, in fact. It was a total surprise for me to find and read it. It drips with sentiment and emotion and a strange, restricted use of words. Women are described as 'females' or 'girls' for example. But that's who I was then.

CELIBACY – A PERSONAL PERSPECTIVE

I write this in the knowledge that in less than five weeks I will be asked if I am willing, freely and irrevocably, to consecrate my life to God through a life of celibacy – I will answer yes. Is it strange, premature, to write on celibacy before making the vow? But the vow itself is merely an affirmation, a public declaration, of a life I am already living. I am a celibate. My perspective is one which has already been coloured by my own interior 'yes' – by my own life history.

I do not want to be a celibate – without a doubt. If I could, I would change this value which has evolved into a tyrannical injustice. I am drawn towards people. I'm not talking about the metaphysical notion that man needs another – at least that's not my explicit aim. I need people. I need their company; I need their affirmation. I need to touch people; I need to make them smile. I need to be allowed to enter into their lives. These 'needs' are not, in my mind, the selfish cries of an infant wanting all the toys on the shelf. I need people for my own wholeness. Can celibacy fulfil this need for me?

In celibacy I am free – just like a butterfly can move from plant to plant – so I can move from person to person. Yet I can never get attached; never say 'this is where I will rest now. The world can pass me by as this is where I belong.' I suppose, in one sense, my need of people will be fulfilled. I will meet more people, make more people smile, touch more people than most others in their life journey. Yet the primary need, that of joining my life with a woman whom I love, can never be fulfilled during a life of celibacy. I must travel alone and that does not make me feel too good.

The last five years of serious celibate commitment have resulted in the minimum of contact with females. Since school they have been a part of my growth which has been cut off at the stem. A serious consequence of this has been the ability to 'fall in love' with every second girl that I have met. This has resulted in various tensions and expressions which have been unfulfilling for me, and probably embarrassing for the girl. Obviously 'love' is something I have not yet known on this one-to-one personal level. By not being allowed to experience real, lasting female company yet 'falling in love' countless times, I feel there is a very real possibility of denigrating 'love' to adolescent infatuation.

In seminary I do not really feel I've been able to overcome the idea of a woman as a sex object. The system has taught me this for it says: see her as an entire person; look at her as a child of God; see her as a unique individual. Yet it also says: do not spend too much time in her company; do not touch her; do not open yourself up to her – for horror of horrors you might both fall in love. But surely falling in love is the basis of the Christian message?

Is falling in love not always going to be a direct consequence of seeking a view of the female which sees her not as an object of my lust – but as a whole person?

Physical expression of my love for someone has, up to now, been non- existent. Yes, perhaps this has been because up to now, I've never really been in love. But perhaps my lack or inability to openly manifest my feelings for a girl because I'm a seminarian, a student priest, has resulted in me shutting off a major part of my person – that part which allows really falling in love to happen?

Celibacy means never experiencing the pleasure of caressing the breast of the girl I love. It involves never allowing our mouths to kiss or our hands to explore.

Celibacy means never being able to tell a girl I love that I love her. Never standing still long enough to hear that she loves me. It involves never having a daughter or a son who I can take into my arms and say, 'You are mine. I love you. I made you. I will always take care of you.'

This makes me inescapably sad. Is love such a bad thing that a priest, a 'love-er', a man who has to wear the badge 'love your neighbour' cannot experience it? Cannot give it?

And what of truth? Am I not to be a bearer of truth? Is my message not to be one of true love? Can I do this if my Church will not allow me to truly love another?

Just now my greatest fear is not 'falling', 'sinning' or 'scandalising'. My greatest fear is that my celibacy – whose aim is to set me free to love – will be the greatest burden to stop me truly loving. Celibacy, for me, is not just 'no sex'. If it is to be valid, I have to be a continually true celibate – that is a true lover.

I fear that this end will be lost amidst a haze of free drink, big meals, parish adulation and total affirmation. I'm afraid that I will fall into a rut of worrying about canonicity and vestments and housekeepers and cars and papal letters and confirmations and parish newsletters. Even celibacy, which I am forced to embrace because of my calling to the priesthood, must never, never, never stand in the way of the true meaning of being a priest.

Ah! the earnest heart and the loneliness of the long-distance, celibate me. Pompous language and the whipped-cream sentimentality aside, there are a number of thoughts in my essay that I am pleased that I found myself making back in 1983. I clearly was immature in my inability to make sound, equal relationships with women. I'm sure that this is true of many priests.

Surprisingly, I do not remember much teaching or psychological formation throughout my time in seminary on actually *being* celibate. I do remember one retreat where the topic of celibacy was raised. The only thing that springs to mind was the old priest saying that you could dress a lamppost with a clerical shirt and collar and some women would throw themselves at it – 'It's not you she wants lads, it's the thought of being with a priest that she's attracted to.'

With vows as a deacon taken, solemn promises made, my life continued much as it had previously, but there was no hiding the power of the step-up that ordained ministry gives you in a seminary. Or out in the parish with people surreptitiously pressing hard-earned folded fivers into your hands and pockets, with a murmured 'A few pounds for yourself, Father'. Having the power of preaching Sunday's sermon at the main Mass in an assigned parish for the first time as a deacon, I experienced what a privileged position a priest has with his people.

I loved being a deacon – this kind of 'mini-priest'. I was now more or less free from Drygrange and could get my sleeves rolled up, and actually practise what I had been training and studying so hard for. That made all the difference. I like to think that I was good at it. People in the parishes that

I served loved me and I loved them back, and I knew, beyond any shadow of a doubt, that things were going to go well for me, that despite everything, I had made the right choices.

I was sent to a parish in the village of Ratho just outside Edinburgh. The priest there had built a wonderful Christian community. The months I spent with him and with the people of that parish were some of the most fulfilling of my life. I was part of a community whose aim was to be a living witness to the power of Jesus' message of love, justice and understanding. Those few months there I truly understood what being a priest is all about.

My last step, ordination to the priesthood, was chalked up for 1 March 1985. It all became a concrete certainty for me now. The finish line was right in front of me, and all I had to do was walk across it.

As the day was approaching, news was breaking that Cardinal Gray was to retire soon, and I and my group would likely be the last priests he would ordain. There were plenty of rumours about who might take over from him, but I gave them little attention. Largely I was distracted, and enjoying myself. There was an ordination to organise. There were relatives to invite, and liturgies to plan.

As well as being a spiritual experience and a religious elevation, my ordination was also my graduation after seven years of hard study and intense emotional journey. When the cardinal anointed my hands, it was as though the referee had stepped into the ring and held my arm aloft. I could walk out of that bout now, and no prof could threaten to expel me, or scrutinise me, or demoralise me, or attempt to humiliate me, or take me into his bedroom because of the hold he had over me. Because I was a priest now. I felt like the champion of the world.

I cannot truthfully say, however, that despite reaching this milestone, I was totally without worry or distraction. This is summed up for me in the scriptural reading I chose for the ceremony. It was from the second chapter of the Book of Ecclesiasticus and it reads:

> My child, if you aspire to serve the Lord, prepare yourself for an ordeal. Be sincere of heart, be steadfast, and do not be alarmed when disaster comes. Cling to him and do not leave him, so that you may be honoured at the end of your days. Whatever happens to you, accept it, and in the uncertainties of your humble state, be patient, since gold is tested in the fire, and the chosen in the furnace of humiliation. Trust him and he will uphold you, follow a straight path and hope in him. You who fear the Lord, wait for his mercy; do not turn aside, for fear you fall.
>
> (Ecclesiasticus 2:1–7.
> *New Jerusalem Bible*, reader's edition)

These words send shivers up my spine as I read them now, because they encapsulate not only my short journey within the priesthood but also my decision to leave it.

'My child, if you aspire to serve the Lord, prepare yourself for an ordeal'. I did aspire to serve the Lord. I loved those early months of being a priest. I enjoyed the intimacy it gave me; the permission to enter into people's lives, often when they were at their lowest point, and somehow to find words or gestures that might help them.

Two aspects of being a priest, in particular, suited me. My short time as a hospital chaplain and, working with people who were grieving: either for their own imminent loss of life, or the loss of someone close to them. Now, I'm a 'frequent flyer' in hospitals due to various health conditions, and am sick of the sight of them. Back at that time though, when I was a temporary part of the chaplaincy team in one of the big hospitals in Edinburgh, I felt that I had found my home. Here was a place where I could really call on the theological resources I had stock-piled during those long years at Drygrange.

As I've said, my main area of academic interest at Drygrange had been in moral theology and, in particular, bioethics. This area essentially covers how people make good choices. People commonly believe that the Church has a stand on life and death issues that is purely black and white. The application of ethics, however, is to see the nuances, the complexities, in such matters. Now I was able to use my knowledge to comfort people who had to make extremely difficult and even life-altering decisions. But more than that, I was able to witness people who were so deeply courageous in coping with life's burdens, and I was truly humbled.

One young man has remained in my memory over the decades. I went to see him one morning on the ward before he was to go down to theatre for his surgery. He told me that he had suffered for years from a condition I had never heard of called Crohn's disease. It sounded absolutely devastating, and an awful thing for anyone to have to live with. 'And your surgery?' I asked.

'Oh, they're going to cut my bowel away and I'm going to get a stoma, Father. I'll be given a bag to attach to my skin to collect my bowel movements in.' I was horrified. It sounded like the one of the worst possible conditions there could be. Of course, life throws up many challenges as time passes. Having suffered three decades of Crohn's-like symptoms, and having exhausted every potential treatment or cure, I ended up with a colostomy and a stoma myself. That young man's courage was later a factor in getting me through – although he'll never know that.

It was in being with people near to death, and through the process of death, that I probably found the purest spiritual reward in my short active ministry. Death is normally a far-off thought when you're in your twenties. But for many patients, nurses, doctors and other staff on the wards I visited it was, of course, a constant presence. I had a short period covering a chaplain's absence at St Columba's Hospice in Edinburgh. I learned about fear and kindness in those places. I learned that death is a process as much as it is an instant. I learned not to fear death, but to accept its inevitability, and in the meantime to try equally to embrace life. Out of all the religious services I prepared at that time, I put the most work into funerals.

A few years ago, I bumped into a dear friend, Caroline Thomson, in Cromarty, a village close to where I live in the Highlands of Scotland. I hadn't seen her for a long time. 'There is something about the finality of death that I can't comprehend,' I said to her. A close relative of hers had recently died and she was sore with the pain of loss. It was a strange thing for me to say to her, and when I returned home

I fretted about why I'd said it. My old dog Molly had just died, and I guess that was on my mind as well as the passing of Caroline's relative.

Eventually I texted her and said something like 'We are so blessed to have you and your family in our lives.' That would not be something I typically would have done. She responded with something so generous and heart-warming. A few days later I got a text from her phone again. This time her husband had written it. He told me that Caroline had been killed in a car crash a few hours previously.

Writing and delivering her eulogy was the hardest thing I've ever done in my life. Being asked to do it was also the biggest privilege anyone has ever given me. I found some degree of strength from the closeness and intimacy with death that I had been exposed to all those years ago when I was a young priest.

In my own way, over the passage of time, I've striven to meet my aspiration to 'serve the Lord'.

* * *

The 'ordeal' foreshadowed by those prescient words from Ecclesiasticus began exactly three months after I was ordained, as I and a fellow priest pal listened to the news on Radio Forth in the parish house of St Margaret Mary's in Granton, Edinburgh. We were waiting for the announcement of who would take over as Archbishop of St Andrews and Edinburgh, following the retirement of Cardinal Gray. The insiders said that it was two-horse race between Mario Conti, the Bishop of Aberdeen, and Keith O'Brien.

When the news came through that O'Brien had been appointed, I knew there was no way I could work in the archdiocese under his leadership. Just twelve weeks into my priesthood I knew that I would have to leave it. It was just a matter of time. Seven years of study and putting up with all that Drygrange offered would be nothing in comparison with the life I would face with O'Brien in charge of my every move.

A priest has no choices when it comes down to his relationship with his bishop. He can't ignore him, and can't challenge him. He's made a vow to obey him and those who follow him. A bishop also sets the tone for the diocese by what he says, by how he preaches, by the company he keeps. I knew too much about O'Brien to know that I could serve as a priest under his governance without betraying my conscience.

* * *

Once the announcement of O'Brien's appointment was made public, his acolytes, those who were now his intimate circle, which of course I was not a part of, were all aflutter. The previous archbishop, Cardinal Gray, had been a remote figure to the younger clergy, but O'Brien had spent years wooing, visiting, and drinking his way round the parish houses of the archdiocese. He made a point of ensuring that he was a well-known face. He was not universally liked by all the clergy, however. Some saw through his whisky-drinking bonhomie and regarded him with suspicion, distaste even. One of the more overtly homosexual priests I knew seemed to see him as a competitor for the affections of another priest they both had their eye on.

We were called to attend his elevation as Archbishop of St Andrews and Edinburgh in the diocesan cathedral. I took in the pomp of the ceremony, the glittering vestments, the mitres, the dignitaries, the faithful watching this glory, and I knew that this was O'Brien's moment of joy. Here was a man who had worked so hard for this day, and now he felt the breath of God on the back of his neck.

5

I STOLE THE ARCHBISHOP'S DINNER

The short note dated 1 August 1985 fell through the letter-box. It was addressed to The Reverend Brian Devlin, and in it I was told that my first official placement was to be the assistant priest in St Ninian's parish in Edinburgh. I was pleased with the appointment. It was based in the city and was a rather unusual parish, that had been organised under Fr Jock Dalrymple. It contained two hospitals: Elsie Inglis Memorial Hospital and the Eastern General Hospital. I knew that I loved hospital work, so this suited me down to the ground.

I moved in a few weeks before Dalrymple was to leave, so I only had a short experience of life in the parish under his leadership. The church house was the centre of the parish. It was one of Edinburgh's historic houses. I always found its Adam design and ornate architecture imposing, and, to be quite honest, it was a creepy place to live in on your own. But the parish made the fullest use of the house possible. It was, quite literally, an 'open' house. There were rooms set aside for homeless people to sleep in overnight.

In all ways the parish house symbolised the biblical notion of welcome and love.

Dalrymple had been a spiritual director at Drygrange too in the past. But he was as different from O'Brien as it is possible to get. This man opened his parish to those who knew best how to run it – the parishioners themselves. St Ninian's had a vibrancy that left all the other parishes in the archdiocese streets behind. Dalrymple was a man from an aristocratic background who slept on the floor of his bedroom because the homeless too slept on the ground; a preacher whose Sunday sermons were so popular that people arrived to Mass early in order to bag a seat; a leader who said that the 'up and ins' were the very people to help the 'down and outs'. He organised the sanctuary of the church building in such a way as to include people, as well as priests – a symbol of the communitarian concept of ministry that was alive and flourishing in St Ninian's.

Practical and symbolic too was the grand sitting-room on the first floor of the house. It was known as the 'Upper Room', reminding everyone of the gospel story where the apostles met Jesus on the way to Emmaus. In St Ninian's, it was the place that the parish met for weekday masses. This hearth of the parish was a warm and welcome place from which no one was turned away. It truly was the epicentre of parish life. Various groups brought vibrancy to the parish and were rooted in that room.

The day that Fr Ian Murray took over as parish priest of St Ninian's was the start of the dismantling of much of the work that Dalrymple had done. Quite literally, the doors to the parish house were locked. People told me of the 'violence' of that locked door. Gone were the meetings, the respite from the rain for the homeless men. Gone too was the Upper Room. Mass would be said every day in the draughty church next door instead.

Murray set about redecorating the house from top to bottom. The best furniture, curtains, bedding and dining sets were purchased from House of Fraser. For me it was certainly much nicer to live in relative luxury than it had been to make do in the busy, chaotic atmosphere of Dalrymple's parish house. But it wasn't worth it. There were now deep divisions within the parish, and I was trying, in my own small way, to mediate a community that was in upheaval. I felt so sorry for those who had lost their identifiable symbol of Christian community.

It's perhaps odd to be able to trace a specific event on a specific day which, innocuous as it seemed at the time, was to be the key which unlocked a new part of my life – a part which would involve leaving the priesthood, entering a new career and making a radical departure from everything I had prepared and worked for, for so long.

One Sunday afternoon Murray and I were to attend a service in St Mary's Cathedral. A nun closely associated with our parish was making a donation to The Leith Group, a local charity helping people who were injecting drug users. The service was to mark the occasion of the donation. The Leith Group itself operated a little way beyond the parish boundary of St Ninian's. This small detail would be an important one a few months later.

I was intrigued by the group. Working with drug users and their families was never particularly an area I had thought about before. Up until then I had been quite happy visiting the hospitals, but the tension that I was feeling within the parish, the feeling of restriction, was causing me real anxiety and stress. I could feel the dark beckoning of depression reach out to me. This feeling was building and was precisely what I had been worried about prior to my ordination and had noted in my paper on my thoughts about celibacy: that I would get caught up in the trivia of parish life, and not really minister to those that I thought I could really help.

Murray felt that one of the important elements of parish work was to visit parishioners, literally knocking on people's doors out of the blue and going in and talking to them. In fairness, that's not an unrealistic expectation for a priest to have. Many of them saw it as a core part of parish life, but the very thought of it would make me shudder with horror. I tried it for a while, but I never embraced it with the enthusiasm that was expected of me. Instead, I was on the lookout for something much more immediately rewarding and interesting.

One afternoon I headed down to the Leith Group. As I walked through the door into a room busy with people in various states of intoxication and the project workers I'd met the previous Sunday, I knew immediately, and without question, that this was where I wanted to be. I asked if they'd have me as a volunteer, and I joined the others in working with these chaotic, bedraggled, invariably poor, often creative and talented, forgotten-about people.

The key project worker in the group was a woman called Alyson. She took me under her wing, and it was from her and the other volunteers, and the drug users themselves, that I learned all I needed to know about the world of heroin addiction in Leith.

Being a contrary figure was to be my downfall with Ian Murray at St Ninian's. Matters like my disinterest in visiting parishioners were becoming more and more problematic for him. But being young and now free from Drygrange, I was determined to do what *I* wanted to do with *my* ministry.

Murray was increasingly agitated about my involvement with the Leith Group, which took me outside the official parish boundary. It became very clear to us both that we were on a collision course and the consequences would be inevitable.

I also bought myself a wee dog, a Jack Russel pup which I named Clyde. I just turned up with her one day. It was a stupid and insensitive, as well as highly impractical, thing to do. The pup did what pups are sent on this earth to do. She peed and crapped on the new carpets and gnawed on the House of Fraser table legs. I was told I had to get rid of her. I gave her to my mum and dad and she lived a long life hunting rabbits in Fife. But getting her was another sign of my increasing thrawnness and childish anger.

Despite my growing feelings of discontent and the shadow of depression, I enjoyed the 'cultic' aspects of Catholic Church life. I liked saying Mass; I embraced the liturgy, which in St Ninian's was almost entirely organised by lay groups and committees. I liked preaching and was, I'd be bold enough to say, courageous and clear in some of my sermons. However, on Remembrance Sunday I can clearly recall counting the months to myself whilst saying Mass, working out how many had passed since my ordination.

I was ordained in March and already by November, I was asking myself when would it not be too early to leave the priesthood. The 'correct' answer of course was never. Ordination to the priesthood involves a commitment until death. Leaving it was a huge source of scandal back in those days. It still is, but perhaps not to the degree it was then. Perhaps that's when thoughts of hastening my death took root.

On a day-to-day level, the new archbishop left me more or less alone. Once I remember he phoned me to ask me to drive him to a parish Mass somewhere. I hated it when this kind of thing happened. I wore a white jacket over my black clerical shirt rather than the customary black suit. A small act of defiance. However, he did have the habit of falling asleep as soon as the journey started, which suited me fine, as I didn't want to talk to him. Having him as my bishop was deeply unsettling. While I never felt any further sexual threat from him, I could never shake off the anxiety I felt being near him or having my life in any sense controlled by him.

Then came the episode of the three meals.

Ian Murray and I had been invited to a parish house off in Fife for a meal with 'the lads'. These meals were a common rubric of priestly life. They were held regularly and were designed to build up a sense of camaraderie between 'brother' priests. They were also an excuse for a complete alcoholic binge. This one was like all of the others: a formal meal with aperitifs, wine and rounded off with spirits. Occasionally the meal would be cooked by the priests themselves; sometimes nuns or a housekeeper or some trusted and discreet women parishioners would prepare, cook and clear up the debris. These get-togethers were terrific fun for the old priests as they regaled us young ones with the japes they had got up to in their time.

The night ended, and Murray bundled himself into the car and I drove home, thankfully sober. I remember distinctly the roundabout in Dunfermline when he belched out his most memorable pearl of wisdom to me. 'I don't understand these guys that leave the priesthood to get married,' he slurred, the topic of priests leaving the ministry having been aired during the meal. 'If they want sex, why don't they visit a massage parlour in Edinburgh, screw one of the prostitutes and then go to Confession the next day? No need to leave.' Fr Ian Murray, who was to be later appointed Bishop of Argyll and the Isles, gazed blearily at me.

And with that I felt it really was time to get ready to go. How easily those words fall onto the page now I write them, but truly, they were breathtakingly difficult to consider at the time. Everything I had done – the years of study and training – would count for nothing. The disappointment and anguish I would cause my family, the shame and vulnerability I would feel, would be unbearable. I would be left with no recognisable qualifications, no job, no house, no income. No certainty of faith. All of these thoughts tumbled around in my mind. But I felt completely and horrifically trapped. If I stayed, I would become even more unhappy. Whatever I did next, I was going to cause untold pain to myself and to others.

The next clerical meal I remember was at St Ninian's itself. About a month previously a very good friend of mine had done the unthinkable, and had left the priesthood. I was raw with anxiety and my nerves were jangling. I missed him badly and, knowing my own perilous position, I was afraid how I'd react if anyone said anything critical about him. Given what was to occur shortly it was a reasonable concern to have.

The chatter around O'Brien, the clerical cliques, life with Ian Murray – who himself told me of his deep distaste for O'Brien – caused dark days and nights for me. I was drinking too heavily and my thoughts were getting bleaker, to the point where I was considering ways I could kill myself without it looking intentional. My need to get out of the priesthood was countered only by the thought of the pain I would cause to those I'd spent my life thus far trying to please.

The guests at the meal included some of Murray's contemporaries. One of them was a high-ranking monsignor who was close to O'Brien. The meal was characterised by the usual badinage, and stories of seminary days were recounted with ever-increasing animation. I was coiled tight, praying that nothing would be said about my pal, and fortunately nothing was mentioned throughout dinner. We ended the night in the Upper Room, which was Murray's huge study now. We sat on the recently purchased House of Fraser leather suite. The party was going swimmingly, and the single malts were smoky and sweet.

Then the monsignor, by this time pretty drunk, decided now was the time to take a pop at my friend who had left the priesthood. I don't remember exactly what he said, but I do remember what the tone of my response was. I was apoplectic with rage. It was a complete and utter explosion that shocked the other guests (it shocked me too, come to that), but it ultimately sealed my fate. It had taken seven long and back-breaking years to become a priest and less than a minute to undo it all.

I will say this in defence of Murray, he did not directly use my behaviour towards the monsignor as his basis for getting rid of me. If he had, I could not really have complained. Undoubtedly though, what happened that night was a sign to him of the distress I was in. What I said was unconscionable, but he saw behind the words a young man in the paroxysms of pain, realising he was coming to the end of his short time as a priest.

A few days later came the inevitable knock on my door and in he came. There was no shouting, no great fuss. It wasn't working, he said. I was not demonstrating sufficient commitment to St Ninian's. The dog had chewed up and peed on the new carpets. I was over involved with the Leith Group, which was not within the parish. I had to decide, he said, whether to give up my contact with the drug group altogether or he would have to contact the archbishop and tell him that I could no longer remain as assistant priest in St Ninian's.

'Don't bother,' I said. 'I'll do it myself. I'll phone him.'

First, though, I had to tell my parents.

I distinctly remember the drive from Edinburgh to their house in Charlestown. I felt that what I was about to do, what I was about to say, was going to be so awful for them, that I would rather die than say it. As I drove onto the motorway leading to the Forth Road Bridge which my father, a steel fixer, had worked long hard years on building, with the cold steel literally frozen onto his poor hands, I wailed. I wanted to be gone. My loving, laughing father would be unable to comprehend how I, who had everything I'd ever asked for, who'd never had to work in the cold, or carry any burden heavier than a book and a pen, was going to throw my life away.

My mum, an archetypal Irish Catholic mother, who had nursed me through my childhood illnesses and who saw in her son's priesthood a glimpse into Heaven itself, whose pride and self-identity was carved into being the mother of a priest, would be crushed.

I wanted – I firmly intended – to kill myself that day. I gunned the car faster and faster. If I could ram it toward a lamp post or a stanchion at high speed my problems would be over. Faster and faster – 60, 70, 80 miles per hour. Tears streamed down my cheeks as I screamed with anguish, despair and guilt: 'Dear Lord, please end this. Jesus Christ, let me go. You're a destroyer, not a father; a tyrant, a killer! Well kill me. Show one bit of yourself and switch me off!'

But He did not. The mercy and end that I sought could never be found like that. Like gold tested in fire, I was to be tested in the furnace of my despair and my humiliation.

What happened afterwards turned out to be every bit as painful and as gut-wrenching as I had imagined it might be. This was to be the start, and not the end, of a book of tears and acrimony and anger. This was to be the beginning of doors being closed, of locks being bolted and of hearts being hardened. I learned a lot – too much. More than anything, I learned that by declaring that I intended to visit O'Brien with a view to leaving the priesthood I was sending myself down a dark road on which I was completely and utterly on my own.

At first, my father couldn't understand why this was all happening. But a few years on he explained that having worked on building sites for most of his life, he'd walked off many a job himself because conditions weren't right. He never judged me, except through the prism of unconditional love. What better aspect exists to view the world from? My mum was understandably devastated; completely and utterly broken by what I was telling her. This had been, after all, what had kept me in Drygrange – this fear of not making it. But, by succeeding and now announcing I was throwing it all away, I had magnified the pain for both of my parents, but particularly for her.

I asked for, and received, a meeting with O'Brien in his residence in Morningside in Edinburgh. St Benet's is an ugly and expensive structure. Its formal gardens are laid out in that part of Edinburgh where 'You'll have had your tea' is the parodied greeting to unwanted visitors. It is unthinkable that O'Brien did not know what I wanted to meet him for. He undoubtedly would have been tipped off by one or other of his senior clergy – a certain hungover monsignor springs to mind – and of course the recent departure from the priesthood of my friend would still have been fresh in his mind.

As was ever the case with O'Brien, there was an atmosphere of bonhomie. Even on occasions such as this. 'Come on in. Sit yourself down. Here, let me get you a drink . . .' The light Irish brogue, the laughter lines around the hazel eyes. Always watching, always alert. He poured an enormous gin for me and a smaller one for himself, and eventually we got round to business.

'I have to leave the priesthood,' I said. I could not live as a priest and serve him dutifully, I continued. It was at this point that arguably I made my most morally questionable mistake in what was a chaotic period in my life, because when he perfectly reasonably asked me why, I did not mention his assault on me in Drygrange. As I've mentioned, since the morning after it happened when he was by my bed as I awoke, we had never discussed it. There had been little time to do so – I had clearly been traumatised, and he had left Drygrange for Blair's shortly after.

Fundamentally, with O'Brien as my bishop, steeped in what I personally experienced to be an ingrained hypocrisy, I knew getting out was going to be essential for my life to have any authentic meaning.

However, I didn't say that. I described my unhappiness at St Ninian's parish; my failed relationship with Ian Murray and my love of working with the injecting drug users in Leith. I needed to leave, I said. I needed to have another life.

I wouldn't describe the meeting as harmonious. Looking at it from O'Brien's perspective – here he was, newly installed into the position of archbishop – he appeared to be unable to keep hold of his newly ordained priests. I was not the last to leave around that time.

My notes of 15 and 17 March 1986 were written in St Catharine's Convent, Lauriston Gardens, in the heart of Edinburgh. I was sent there for a month under mutual agreement that I would take some time out to definitively decide whether or not I really wanted to leave the priesthood. It would be a big decision, and not one that could be reversed. I think my notes convey what was going on in my mind at the time.

SATURDAY 15 MARCH

I'm trying to decide – I am lonely – I am afraid – I don't want to hurt – I don't want to 'have a vocations crisis'. I am afraid – I am lonely.

I want to find out exactly what I have to do with my life. Coming here I feel is like owning up to having AIDS . . . I feel like I'm waiting for the rush – already I've had two phone calls from parishioners – both fucking lunatics, both trying to find out [what has happened].

'What went wrong, Brian?' says Keith. 'What went wrong on your course . . . you can't handle the pressure. Did they not tell you there'd be pressure?

Look at me, I've got pressure – I'm not weak – well . . . we're all weak. But get close to Jesus. He's strong and you're weak and if you stand close to Him you'll be strong too.'

'It seems simple when you put it like that, Keith.'

My note of that day continues: 'I want so much to become a happy person again. I am not happy just now because I feel horribly trapped in this priestly cloak.'

Looking back now, 15 March 1986 must have been a rough day. Two days later wasn't a lot better. I wrote:

MONDAY 17 MARCH
Today I feel worried regarding my immediate future. I am afraid that I will be 'on the street'. I do not want to go back to a parish ever again. I am afraid of poverty – but maybe that's because I've not really considered the price of freedom. Today I began to doubt my talents to even exist in this world. But I have got a lot, I realise that – just, is it enough? Basically, I feel insecure and lacking in confidence.

The Leith Group is therapeutic for me – [but] today I'd be no good to an addict – or tomorrow.

It's been a beautiful spring weather day – sunshine and warm. I started walking to Restalrig – very noble – but gave up after 200 yards and got a taxi. I'll have to stop all this weakness.

When I wrote that I was afraid of poverty, that I'd be out on the street, this was no mere poetic reflection. I literally did not know how I would survive, how I would get a job. How could I describe myself to a future employer? Where would I live? I couldn't go back to Charlestown. A few kind and loving friends did offer me a couch. But ultimately I felt on the brink of being one of the 'down and outs' that used to visit St Ninian's before the doors were locked. It was, I believed at the time, a very real possibility.

The weeks passed quickly and the Sisters of Mercy in the convent were, by and large, very kind to me. They left me to my own devices. Most of my time was spent trying to find a flat, being unsuccessful in looking for work, and finding out about how to sign on to the social security system.

At the end of the month O'Brien asked me what I had decided, and I outlined my plan to leave. It was all pretty uneventful really. There was no breakdown. No tears were shed, nor breasts beaten. In fact, it was quite perfunctory. We talked money. I had none. He had loads. Clearly, I would need some cash, I said, for the down payment for my rented flat, which would be paid through housing benefit. I also asked him for money for food and accessories until my benefit money was agreed. It was all rather embarrassing, both for him and for me. In all I was given £580 from diocesan funds, plus a £200 personal cheque from him. I was also told that my National Insurance contribution would cease to be paid by the archdiocese from the day I left the convent.

With the discussion over, we moved to the dining table and a meal was served and the wine was poured. At the start of the main course the phone rang. I remember this clearly because it was the first time I had ever seen a cordless telephone. It lay on the table and O'Brien picked it up. I have no doubt at all, prior to that day, he'd have carried on his conversation with me in the room, unless it had been seriously confidential. This time however, with ostentation he arose from his seat, and phone to his ear, he left the room. I was no longer part of the brotherhood.

I was alone in the archbishop's dining room. I ate my steak and chips. He had been gone now for a good five minutes. I poured another glass of claret. I sat in silence. I was edgy. I'd nearly finished my meal, but his was practically untouched. Six, seven minutes passed. I eyed his plate. I thought 'I don't know when I'll see a plate of food like this again' and cut a good two-thirds off his steak and half his chips and put them onto my plate and devoured them. When eventually he did return, he looked at his own plate, saw that mine was empty and suggested it was time for me to go. It was my last supper.

I was shown to the door of St Benet's for the last time as a priest. This time no taxi was called for me. I was on my own now. With a cursory handshake, and no embrace, I was gone, and my official priesthood was over. I walked into the spring night air with a mixed heart but a full belly.

The powers that a priest has to carry out his sacramental duties are called 'faculties'. These are bestowed by the bishop and can be removed by the bishop. O'Brien wrote to me on 29 April 1986. His letter concluded:

> As I further indicated to you on Saturday evening, as from the time when you leave St Catherine's convent to occupy your flat, I am withdrawing your Archdiocesan Faculties. These include faculties to say Mass, hear Confession, preach and administer the Sacraments – unless [sic] the Anointing of the Sick in case of emergency.

With this statement my ministerial priesthood ceased.

But he had a favour to ask. A favour, which when you look at things from the perspective of hindsight, was rather perverse, but telling:

> One favour I would ask of you is that you do not unduly influence any of our Diocesan students for the Priesthood. I am aware that influences from former Priests may have been exerted on you, and I would not like this to happen in any further cases.

This need for O'Brien to pin the blame on outside 'influences' is a typical reaction of the Church hierarchy in so many spheres. Especially in those days, it blamed social disintegration, sexual permissiveness, intrinsic evil, feminism, the growth of the left, the abandonment of the natural law, a questioning media, lack of respect for the clergy, the breakdown of the nuclear family unit. Only relatively lately have they been forced, largely with great reluctance, to look inwards and see what others have seen and known for years - that the chief influence for the failures of the Church to be relevant in society lies within their own ranks. It lies with the brotherhood which has been corrupted by lies and by cruelty.

6

DID THE PRIESTHOOD EVER
REALLY LEAVE ME?

My first proper job after closing the door on my parish was as a project worker with the Leith Group, where I had volunteered as a priest. Most of the drug users that my colleagues and I worked with took heroin as their drug of choice – if they had much of a choice – and injecting as their means of administration. I loved that job. The clients were a mixed group of people – mostly poor and many ravaged by the effects that their lifestyle was having on them. They brought me face to face with need and suffering in a way that I had never previously encountered.

In the mid-1980s, Edinburgh had earned an unwanted soubriquet. In an article in *The Independent* of 5 August 1994 the extent of the problem was retrospectively summarised:

> Deaths due to drug overdoses predominated throughout the early 1980s in injecting drug users, but the impact of HIV infection, contracted largely through sharing needles and some heterosexual sex, is now being felt.

A crackdown by Scottish police on drug users in the early days of the AIDS epidemic forced addicts to share needles, and accelerated the spread of the virus. Edinburgh became known as the AIDS capital of Europe.

The virus was claiming the lives of so many young, vulnerable people in Scotland's capital city. Already hated, reviled and feared, these infected heroin users became even more of a safe target for a frightened and confused public to vent their anger towards. Our job was to help these addicts to reduce harm to themselves and others. A tough job it was. Many of our clients, despite our best efforts, spent time in a range of Scottish prisons. We were there to visit them and to advocate for them as best we could. Many of the female clients were also prostitutes, some of them working the streets late at night, often forced out there by their addicted male partners. Our job was to try to convince them to make sure their clients wore condoms. How many did?

We had to teach ourselves about HIV so that we in turn could educate our clients and the wider population on how the virus could be spread and how it could be avoided. I was absolutely clear in my mind that, barring some catastrophe, there was no way that I was at risk of becoming infected myself. That didn't stop me from breaking into a cold sweat once though, when a young man who I knew to be HIV positive lit a cigarette in his mouth and passed it to me as I drove him somewhere in my car. For a brief second, I faltered. That cigarette might kill me. But I wasn't thinking of lung cancer.

Over a year later I was approached to join an organisation called Scottish AIDS Monitor (SAM). This was a body that had been started up by some very brave and visionary gay men in the city. The so called 'gay plague' meant that a huge swathe of people were demonised as being the carriers of death and pestilence into civilised society. I was brought into SAM because of the experience I'd gained in the Leith Group around the particular manifestation of the epidemic in Edinburgh. My job there was to be the National Training and Counselling Officer, and one of my tasks was to grow and develop a system of support called Buddy Counselling, for people with full-blown AIDS or who were simply HIV positive. Here volunteers were trained to befriend and partner-up with people who had the disease. We extended this into some of Scotland's prisons as many of our clients were still housed there.

It was ground-breaking and often heart-breaking work. Despite the seriousness of the issues, the constant anger from portions of the public and the media, and inevitably the background noise of the Catholic Church preaching about condoms not being the answer and abstinence being the only sure protection from this virus, it was a place of real compassion, humour and acceptance. And profound tenderness. Those were the days when Princess Diana sitting beside, and shaking hands with, people with AIDS caused a global headline. It all seems so far away now. But, in reality, it is still within touching distance.

My AIDS work took me to the Highlands in 1989 and I became the area's first HIV prevention officer. I detected a sense that those in polite circles up here felt that the virus wouldn't make it up the main trunk road from Edinburgh. Somehow it would become exhausted by the hike through the mountains, and would contain itself in the more 'sinful' parts of Scotland.

Our problem in the Highlands was apathy, and my job was to shake people out of that. My first campaign was entitled: AIDS: Talk about It. We produced posters and leaflets and imported vast numbers of condoms, many of them flavoured. We even produced beer mats with an AIDS message on both sides, one side in Gaelic. We agreed somewhere down the line that AIDS was spelt the same in Gaelic as it was in English.

But our struggle to find a platform to get real debate and discussion going was huge, until we thought of something rather clever. Effectively my boss, and certainly my champion, was Caroline Thomson, whom I mentioned earlier. She was a member of the Health Board, and was fearless in her determination to get things done. I was quite a junior person in the Health Board, but she directed me through the bureaucracy and gave me permission to be as creative as possible. So, our leaflets became slightly raunchier and our posters a little bit 'saucier'.

We had a discussion one day about our marketing strategy. We wanted AIDS talked about, but, in reality, the only sector who were making any noise in the Highlands were the churches, though not in a way that was effective. So, we decided to take them on directly. We invited them all to a conference about AIDS in Inverness. It's impossible here to describe the frothing at the mouth and the gnashing of teeth that went on at that conference and the subsequent meetings we held. From memory I think we had, or at least invited, all of the Christian tribes – the Catholics, the Church of Scotland, the Episcopalians, the Free Church, the United Free Church, the Free Presbyterians, the Associated Presbyterians, various Baptists, the Salvation Army, the Methodists and the Pentecostalists. People in the Highlands seemed to speak about nothing but AIDS once that particular fire was lit. Someone told me afterwards that their memory of these endeavours was that they were courageous and respectful. They were also exhausting.

In Caroline's eulogy I recounted her wisdom, her fierce determination and her charm. I also told the attendees at the service about our work with the churches, and how at one point towards the end of the day of the conference I turned to her and whispered, 'You know what?'

'What?' she whispered back.

'We have created an ecumenical miracle. Never since the reformation has the Christian Church been as united as it is today – in their outright condemnation of us.' Caroline rocked back in her chair, and hooted with laughter.

* * *

Many years later, I was interviewed on a television programme once about what it had been like to leave the priesthood – this was long before the O'Brien story broke. It was a time when being an 'ex-priest' was more newsworthy than it is nowadays. The questions were probing, and I thought I handled them fairly well. The format was just me and the interviewer – Catherine Deveney – and it was 'as live'. In other words, although it was recorded, there wasn't really any way of stopping it if I made an idiot of myself.

So, it took quite a bit of concentration. Deveney is a skilled interviewer, and I found out just how skilled when she came to her 'and finally, Brian' question. I can't remember the exact wording now, but it was along the lines of 'Has part of you never stopped being a priest?' Talk about going into an emotional tailspin.

Up until then I had presented myself as having a bit of an icy disengagement from the Church. That question knocked me for six. I asked Catherine afterwards if my discomfort was noticeable, and she reassured me that I had coped with it well. I can't even remember now how I did answer. But it is a question that I've thought about a lot over the years.

Leaving all the theological and canonical stuff aside, there is a deeper question to be answered. Am I still a priest? Not in the strict sense of saying Mass, or preaching, or celebrating marriages, obviously, but in a deeper, more personal way?

I wrote earlier about my journey into and out of faith when I was in Drygrange. Those doubts used to plague me with worry and with anxiety. If there is no God and there is no after-life, then what a bloody waste of time my life has been. I wonder how my life might have been so different if I had done what I was good at, and studied English or history at university. What might I have achieved? Where might I be now?

But that's not a helpful way of thinking. As I sit writing this, I look out of my window at the Moray Firth estuary. To the right are the tops of the Cairngorm mountains. My old dog, Minnie, snores at my feet and I can see a pair of wood pigeons carrying twigs in their beaks to build their nest just as they did this time last year. I have to be honest and say that in so many ways my life has been blessed by something.

Whether it be good fortune, or a very attentive guardian angel, I don't know.

I have tended to see my life in two parts: before and after I 'left the priesthood'. The question though is, has the priesthood ever left me?

No, is the truthful answer. The priesthood never left me, because in amongst all of my doubt about faith and an afterlife I do think that the historical Jesus – the man who thought and worked and fought with authorities, the man who made a radical option for the poor and the downtrodden, and the person who actively sought out the company of those society shunned, that contrary man – taught me many lessons. Lessons which I have put to use in my work with drug abusers and in AIDS awareness and with others who have been bullied or victimised over the years.

7

DISCERNMENT

I finally gave in to my resistance to opening a Facebook account one day in 2010. Basically, being easily distracted and a bit nosey, I wanted to see what the fuss was all about. After a quiet start I enjoyed the interactions with people. Names kept appearing, 'friend requests' were made and received, and in a few days I was a committed Facebooker.

Whilst logged in one day, I came across a priest that I had known from before. I'll call him 'Andy'. This appealing, intelligent man and I jumped immediately into conversation about the past, using the private message facility. Having had my faculties removed by O'Brien decades previously did not dampen one particular priestly trait: the pursuit and sharing of gossip. It was a great treat to hear all the old news. Out of the blue, Andy commented, almost in passing, that O'Brien was in trouble for having allegedly sexually assaulted a priest, and that he was under some sort of investigation by the authorities in Rome. The episode was said to have happened when he had been sent to Rome to receive his cardinal's red hat from Pope John Paul II in 2003.

On hearing this my heart almost exploded in my chest. I could hardly take in what Andy was telling me. That morning decades before – the morning after O'Brien had sexually assaulted me in his bedroom after night prayer, when he stood ashen-faced by my bed and told me how sorry he was

I couldn't make any assumptions about whether what he did to me was a 'one off' or not. Now I knew that I was not alone. Some official complaint had been made about him, and he had been found out.

Tentatively I began to tell Andy what O'Brien had done to me in Drygrange, and immediately he responded saying he'd rather speak to me on the phone than communicate through Facebook. What followed were a series of long and harrowing conversations during which I heard in detail how systematically O'Brien had abused my friend.

Undoubtedly, bumping into Andy online had been completely down to chance. Then Andy put me in touch with 'Tony' and 'Paddy' – both of whom were also ministering priests I had known and who had suffered abuse at the hands of O'Brien. It was almost too astonishing to believe that, after never having spoken to these men for decades, we were now having deep and intimate conversations about similar experiences from the past which had caused us immense suffering.

I am not able to speak on anyone else's behalf; only my own. But I will say this – the interaction I had with Andy, Tony and Paddy delivered me, to some significant degree, the antidote to O'Brien. We were all strong men, independently proud and capable, but who had felt diminished, saddened and lessened by O'Brien.

Kind, warm, funny and honest, those three men showed me true friendship. They did not see what had happened to me as being less relevant than their experiences because I had left the priesthood and they'd stayed and slogged it out. Instead, they embraced me and reminded me that, amongst the squalor and the grime that infects the corridors of power of much of the Catholic Church, there exists beauty, perspicacity and heroism.

As I mentioned earlier, I had known the award-winning journalist Catherine Deveney for many years. We both lived in the same area and we worked on many stories together when she was working for national newspapers and I was in charge of Highland Health Board's press office (meaning for a large part I *was* the Health Board's press office). She is a good friend, as well as a trusted journalist.

I set about trying to convince Andy, Tony and Paddy that the right thing to do was to trust Catherine, and to tell their story anonymously to the media. On reflection, I must have made a complete nuisance of myself with the other three men, such was my conviction that 'going public' was the right thing to do. After all, here were three priests who were not free to do what they wanted; who were ministering away in parishes, and whose lives were built around the priesthood. The PR professional in me, as well as the person now outraged by the extent of O'Brien's dishonesty, wanted to go for the jugular through public exposure.

But then something occurred which took the story into an entirely different direction than I could ever have imagined. One of the priests, Paddy, phoned me one night. Paddy, who I knew to be a deeply prayerful, gentle and reflective man, wanted to follow an internal Church route into pursuing a complaint against O'Brien. This route, it transpired, involved contacting the papal ambassador, or Nuncio as he is known in the Church, Archbishop Antonio Mennini. Paddy suggested that he knew a priest – who I'll call 'Fr Mackay' – whom he trusted to tell Mennini of our concerns about O'Brien, in order to set the process in motion to deal with our complaint.

Eventually, and not altogether happily, I agreed to this course of action. Fr Mackay would contact Mennini on our behalf, but would make it clear that we were prepared to take this matter to the media if Mennini did not address it seriously. With the benefit of hindsight, this was an inspired decision that was to test almost to the limit whether the Church actually had an internal process that could be relied on to take such complaints seriously.

Looking back on the correspondence about this early stage of the saga, I'm reminded of how courageous these priests were to take this step. I emailed Fr Mackay on the 6 February 2013, indicating that I was one of the four men that he had been told were complaining about O'Brien's inappropriate behaviour. I needed clarity on how to actually make my complaint.

Within a few minutes I received this response:

Dear Brian,
Thanks for your email. It's good to hear from you, although not good about the circumstances. I feel dreadful for you and the others.
    You can either send the statement directly to the Nuncio, or send it to me and I shall forward it with

an enclosed letter. I shall probably be writing to him today and can mention that another statement will be coming. If you send it to me or to the Nuncio, you do need to send a hard copy with your signature on it.

Please include at the end of your statement before your signature something like the following:

I swear before amighty [sic] God that all the information I have given in this statement is complete and true.

You are very much in my prayers.

Best wishes

The typo in his line about swearing before 'amighty God' makes me smile. I was to wonder in the weeks and months ahead whether God actually had a place in any of the to-ing and fro-ing of trying to get the Church, even fractionally, to show due process regarding our complaint. It was to prove important, however, to follow the process that Fr Mackay had laid out before us. In the meantime, my own response to the email was short and included this thought:

Yes. Sad times and hurt lives. No-one knows what suffering goes on. And a lot of it went on in Drygrange I fear which is why some of us ended up as we did.
Regards
Brian

Looking back on my correspondence with Fr Mackay during the course of writing this book has been a somewhat dispiriting exercise. Not because of anything to do with him.

He was to prove himself to be a courageous and kind man to me during what was to follow.

No. What is dispiriting is how much real fear I felt once we had made our decision to complain about O'Brien. I had written my letter to the Nuncio in which I outlined what my relationship with O'Brien had been in the early days of the seminary and what he did to me. It was clear, factual and uncompromising.

> I then wrote to Fr Mackay after sending him a copy of the letter:
>
> Thank you [I wrote on 7 February] for your kindness and your pastoral concern on this matter. I have real worries about the ramifications for those involved once these land on the Nuncio's desk.
>
> In a spirit of fraternal sharing, I am happy for you to view the letter that I am sending to the Nuncio today. I'd appreciate your confidentiality surrounding it. Any thoughts on it, and how it might be received, would be gratefully welcome.

I suppose I was going through something akin to 'buyer's remorse'. At the time I felt that this was the most dangerous part of the process. The letters we had sent to the Nuncio relied on him handling the situation with haste, with sensitivity and with honesty. Fr Mackay's response to me, about seven hours later, did not fill me with optimism:

> Thanks for sending the attached to me. I feel so sorry for you and all that you have been through. I appreciate your worries about making known your

experiences – however, I do believe that the Nuncio will respect confidentiality.

He is a good man who has a sense that all is not right in the archdiocese, and I am confident will do his utmost to sort matters out. I only hope he can convince all the powers that be in Rome to go along with this, but I think the threat of a public scandal might make matters move very quickly.

There are some very important observations in this response that are worth reflecting on.

The Pope's representative in the United Kingdom already suspected that something was amiss in the archdiocese, and he tolerated that risk. Presumably this knowledge that the Nuncio had would have been connected to the complaint he had already received from the priest O'Brien harassed in Rome when he was made cardinal? I didn't know for sure, but he already knew something wasn't right. Fr Mackay described the Nuncio as a 'good man', yet he was prepared to allow O'Brien to continue ministering as a cardinal in Scotland. Of course, he may have had in mind that O'Brien had tendered his resignation as archbishop already, as he was legally bound to do at the age of seventy-five, and so would slip quietly into the shadows.

But hang on. That couldn't work. O'Brien would still have been a cardinal. That meant he would have a duty to attend any further conclave to elect the next pope until he reached eighty years of age. He'd still have an enormous public profile. Still be Scotland's number one Catholic. No, the key to understanding Nuncio Mennini's tolerance lies in the next bit of text that Fr Mackay wrote: 'I only hope he [Mennini] can convince all the powers that be in Rome to go along with this, but I think the threat of a public scandal might make matters move very quickly.' We took that to mean the threat of bad publicity would be enough to get an immediate reaction. How wrong we were.

Fr Mackay was showing remarkable perspicacity with this comment. It was not enough for four priests to swear before a mighty God and testify that they were abused by O'Brien for any meaningful action to be taken. Very far from it. Instead the Nuncio would have to 'convince all the powers that be in Rome' to take our concerns on. And the only thing that might convince them to take action quickly – or perhaps any kind of action at all – was the threat of a very public scandal. This is what they got eventually, and as will soon become apparent, it was triggered by Nuncio Mennini's own mishandling of the situation.

This petrified me. I had not at all considered that the Church might choose to do nothing. I had never for an instant thought that anyone would need to be convinced. I had presumed that there would be some sort of legal process that the Church would have in place to deal with whistle-blowers like us, and it wouldn't matter if the person being accused was a priest, bishop or cardinal. I was very wrong. The fact is, no process existed within the Church for a situation like ours. The mantra would be repeated over and over: only the Pope can deal with a cardinal. If O'Brien had been a mere priest, what *should* have happened is that he'd have been suspended pending an inquiry. However, we know enough now about how the Church handles such processes, in the light of the child abuse horror show, to know that bishops have continually played fast and loose with such procedures.

This is though, an important lesson for others to learn when they have an argument to make with Church authorities. Depending on the nature of the issue, it is probably never enough to merely present the facts within some sort of closed forum. Combining that with the blaze of public scrutiny is, in my experience, often a necessary action to take.

My letter to the Nuncio was dated 7 February 2013. As I pointed out earlier it was made clear to Fr Mackay that the Nuncio should be under no illusions whatsoever that if there were not a response to our testimonies within a very short period of time, the matter would be handed over to a journalist.

There was no immediate response from Nuncio Mennini.

However, something truly momentous did happen. Something so unexpected it left much of the Catholic world rocking on its heels.

The Pope resigned.

For the first time in 600 years a Pope exited stage left. There had been rumours of reports about massive problems in the Vatican. The Pope's butler, Paolo Gabriele, leaked secret papers to a journalist, highlighting some of the problems that his master faced. Pressure was building on the old man deep in the Vatican.

The news broke when I was in the bath with the radio on. I was listening to a programme on Irish radio when the host, Pat Kenny, broke the news. I nearly drowned in my attempt to get to the radio to turn the volume up. With water dripping around my feet, I stood on the bathroom floor and listened in amazement. It was true. The Pope had resigned, and there was to be a call to all the cardinals of the world to gather in Rome to elect his successor. Presumably, O'Brien would have to attend. It's what cardinals are for - to elect a new Pope.

What a colossal hypocrisy this was. Were the retiring Pope, the Nuncio and senior cardinals in Rome going to allow O'Brien, whom they knew to be an accused sexual predator, to participate in the election process of the next pontiff? Clearly, the chances of him being picked for the job would be slim. But they were not zero – the college of cardinals is not a big pool.

As the news sunk in, we learned that Benedict was to slip quietly into the background to live a secluded life of prayer and reflection. With the announcement of his resignation so soon after our sending in sworn testimonies of complaint against O'Brien, amongst all the anxiety I also felt a sense of confused fascination. I didn't think our intervention had, in itself, precipitated Benedict's resignation, but I did wonder whether it might have been a contributing factor.

And still we waited to hear from the Nuncio. The silence was causing paroxysms of anxiety within me.

The media were outlining how the next Pope was to be appointed. Prior to the secret conclave itself there was to be a series of pre-conclave meetings – or general congregations – during which the cardinals could address the state of the Church amongst themselves, and discuss the sort of attributes the new Pope must have.

One night, on the evening TV news in Scotland, up popped O'Brien. Sitting in front of an altar, he spoke of his plans to attend the forthcoming conclave. He mused on the possibility of a non-European Pope, even one hailing from a developing country. He was his usual carefree, twinkle-eyed self. My reaction on seeing how he conducted himself in that interview was the feeling you might get if a twenty-stone rugby player took a run up of ten yards and crushed you right in the chest with all his might.

By now I was beginning to feel the Church was playing with us, that they had no intention whatsoever of dealing with our complaint seriously. I had allowed myself to be convinced that giving them the option of putting in place some sort of process was a sensible approach. I remember feeling furious with myself. I wrote in an email to one of the priests that 'Waiting for this Nuncio to get back to me is like waiting for the man to fix the boiler. Endless. Feckin' pissed off now.'

I had been misguided to think that O'Brien would be made to look us in the eye and answer us - it had been one of our hopes that we would have some sort of 'truth and reconciliation' process. However, to get to the period of reconciliation we first had to learn the truth. We had to understand what O'Brien's defence was and why he had behaved in the way he did towards each of us.

Eventually, the outrage that we expressed to Fr Mackay about lack of progress forced the Nuncio to act. Fr Mackay was invited to London to meet with Mennini. What the Nuncio decided next was the spark that almost torched the Catholic Church in Scotland. We were informed by Fr Mackay that first of all Mennini appreciated our 'courage' in writing what we had. Never before had the word 'courage' taken on a more sinister tone.

We were informed that Mennini had judged it best to allow O'Brien to go to Rome as planned 'because that would make it easier to arrange his retirement to be one of prayer and seclusion like the Pope'. Finally, the warning came: 'If news of all this becomes public, immense furher [sic] damage is going to be done to the Church, and we shall have even more pieces to pick up.'

By warning us of the consequences of going public, Fr Mackay was telling us that the fallout to the Church, and the subsequent scandal, would cause people to question their very faith. I knew this very well, as my faith had been shaken to the core that morning when I looked at O'Brien's face in the chapel after he'd apologised to me for his behaviour the previous evening.

I strongly believe that Mennini's decision that O'Brien should travel to Rome was a huge error of judgement. It sparked a whole flurry of questions in our little group. Would O'Brien ever come back? Would we hear that he had been given a job and an apartment there to last him into his dotage? If that were the case, would that not give the impression to the faithful in Scotland that he'd been given some miraculous reward and promotion by the Vatican after a long and exemplary career? The Vatican did have form in this area. Another famous prelate, Cardinal Bernard Law, fled his Boston diocese in 2002 over charges of cover-up of child abuse by members of his clergy. In 2004 Pope John Paul II appointed him to the exalted position of Archpriest of the Basilica of St Mary Major in Rome.

All of those questions were bouncing around. Mennini, and I suspect Fr Mackay, did not believe that we would do what we ended up doing: taking the matter out of their hands and exposing O'Brien's story to the blaze of public scrutiny.

There were many frenzied and concerned emails and calls between the members of our group about our next step. We recognised that going public, through the media, was the nuclear option. Once done we could not fully predict the outcome. But, on the other hand, as long as our testimonies were only in the hands of Church authorities we were facing an unknown risk (especially the priests who were still in active ministry), and I was certain that the Church would default to saving its own face for the avoidance of scandal.

In the midst of it all Catherine Deveney acted with the highest ethical standards. She never pressurised us. She understood what it meant for all the individuals concerned. Right up to the final minute she waited until she had complete agreement.

The leading headline in *The Observer* Internet edition on 23 February 2013 was to the point: 'UK's top Cardinal accused of "inappropriate acts" by priests':

> Three priests and a former priest in Scotland have reported the most senior Catholic clergyman in Britain, Cardinal Keith O'Brien, to the Vatican over allegations of inappropriate behaviour stretching back 30 years.
>
> The four, from the diocese of St Andrews and Edinburgh, have complained to Nuncio Antonio Mennini, the Vatican's ambassador to Britain, and demanded O'Brien's immediate resignation. A spokesman for the Cardinal said last night that the claims were contested.

Deveney's pen was as sharp and precise as I knew it would be.

I gave a couple of quotes to help readers of the story have an insight into how I felt about O'Brien at the time. One of them explained the power balance between a priest and his bishop.

> 'You have to understand,' explains the ex-priest, 'the relationship between a bishop and a priest. At your ordination, you take a vow to be obedient to him. He's more than your boss, more than the CEO of your company. He has immense power over you. He can move you, freeze you out, bring you into the fold ... he controls every aspect of your life. You can't just kick him in the balls.'

In effect, though, that is what we had done. The wincing, tear-inducing, sick-making pain that comes with such an action was just beginning to be felt. I sat in my armchair as the story gained traction and watched the television news. Twitter was my companion that night. Very quickly the news began to spread. As the world woke up, the story was now global.

We were informed after the news broke that the Nuncio was 'not happy at all' and was travelling north to see us all, but the next day the meeting was called off. Fr Mackay wrote: 'The Nuncio was in contact with me again yesterday evening. There will be further developments tomorrow, but he will not be coming to Scotland himself. He asks me to pass on the gratitude of Cardinal Ouellet of the Congregation for Bishops for your courage.'

There's that word 'courage' again. Depending on your perspective, it can be interpreted in a number of ways. Cardinal Ouellet runs the Congregation for Bishops. He is a very powerful man in the Catholic Church. His is the department that appoints bishops and arranges visits from Bishops' Conferences all over the world to meet with the Pope. A Canadian, he was considered *papabile* – a hot favourite to be appointed pope. I may be wrong, but there was a lot going on for Ouellet at the time. Popes don't resign often. Conclaves must be hard to organise. He might become Pope himself. I find it hard to imagine that as he read the news that four priests had gone public on the sexual predation of one of his cardinals to a newspaper like *The Observer*, his first thought was of our 'courage'. My own opinion is that he was alerting us to his fury, outrage and severe displeasure at our insubordination. We had exposed a massive scandal at the heart of the Church, and 'scandal' as we will soon explore, has a very significant meaning to the clergy. Avoidance of it is the fig leaf that they use to cover up enormous harm.

The story was running now. It was time for various commentators to share their insights into these revelations. On 26 February 2013, Professor Tom Devine wrote about it in *The Herald*. Devine is a historian of high renown and speaks often to the media. He talked about his personal sadness about the turn of events and his human concern for the cardinal. In the same piece he said: 'This is probably the gravest single public crisis to hit the Catholic Church in Scotland since the Reformation, and its effects in the short term are incalculable. Many of the faithful in Scotland will be stunned by the seismic turn of events and left demoralised.'

As for us, those whose story Deveney had broken, he said:

> . . . in the cause of transparency and indeed fairness to all, it is time for Cardinal O'Brien's anonymous accusers to step forward into the public domain. If Catholicism in Scotland is to move on from this tragic affair a number of serious questions urgently require frank and honest answers from all concerned. The nation's Catholics deserve nothing less.

I was told that he did, subsequently, soften that line. I was grateful to hear that because the statement he made was immensly hurtful and damaging at the time. We were not 'anonymous accusers'; not to those who *needed* to know who we were. It's true our names were not in the public domain, but we used the process given to us to seek justice and truth – and yes even, sometime in the future, reconciliation – in relation to O'Brien. Fr Mackay knew who we were, the Nuncio and Cardinal Ouellette knew us. Even the Pope knew who we were. That was the chain of command. We chose to follow the path the Church asked us to. The fact that the Church made that path impossible for us wasn't our fault.

As I've outlined, Church authorities were blinded by their fear of scandal. The true scandal though, wasn't the publicity that we directly caused. The scandal was the hypocritical sexual predation of Cardinal O'Brien and the desire, in the full knowledge of that behaviour, by Church leaders to quietly cover it up. Like the case of the seminarian in Drygrange, when students and staff had been told not to talk about his suicide, silence and cover-up results in no lessons being learned. All the evidence of scandals in the Church around the world is that, for the sake of all, the Church needs to learn from when things go badly wrong.

On 25 February 2013, the day after the story broke in the print edition of *The Observer*, the BBC reported a statement from O'Brien. His retirement that he had already submitted earlier the previous year – as he was bound by Church law to do – had been accepted by the Pope and was to begin from that day:

> Approaching the age of seventy-five and at times in indifferent health, I tendered my resignation as Archbishop of St Andrews and Edinburgh to Pope Benedict XVI some months ago.
>
> I was happy to know that he accepted my resignation *nunc pro tunc* [now for then] on 13 November 2012. The Holy Father has now decided that my resignation will take effect today, 25 February 2013, and that he will appoint an apostolic administrator to govern the archdiocese in my place until my successor as Archbishop is appointed.

The Church's media spokesman in Scotland, Peter Kearney, commented on the chronology of events on the evening news a few days later. He was asked by the TV reporter whether the acceptance of O'Brien's previously submitted resignation was unrelated to the *Observer* story a few days previously:

'That's right. It isn't related. The timescale the . . . the decision to accept that resignation has not been influenced by the articles that appeared on Sunday.

The timing is very, very unfortunate and it does appear as if one has followed the other, which in terms of chronology one has followed the other, but that's not the same as saying one was caused by the other.'

Public relations is, I'd argue, more art than science. Having practised it for many years in the NHS, I have learned that the art is often in knowing when to say nothing. Or to admit that 'yes, it does look bad doesn't it?' Public relations students would do well to study the entire media handling of the O'Brien case by the Church's press office. I'll leave it for others to decide whether their handling of it belongs in the 'how-best-to-do-it' or 'how-not-to-do-it' category.

I remember deeply reflecting on these statements by Devine and Kearney over the following days, so when Deveney contacted me to ask what the week had been like and how the Church's response had made me feel, on the back of their comments, I was more than happy to respond for the next edition of *The Observer* which was published on the evening of Saturday 2 March:

> He [that is me, the ex-priest] is 'disappointed' by the 'lack of integrity' shown by the Catholic church. 'There have been two sensations for me this week. One is feeling the hot breath of the media on the back of my neck and the other is sensing the cold disapproval of the church hierarchy for daring to break ranks. I feel like if they could crush me, they would,' he told the *Observer*.
>
> He added that he was shocked when Peter Kearney, director of communications for the church in

Scotland, claimed O'Brien's resignation was not linked to the *Observer* story and that the church did not know the details of the allegations.

He said he felt particularly angered by demands that the identity of the four complainants be revealed: 'To those who want to know my name I would say, what does that change? And what do you think I have done wrong?'

He said that when the four came forward to the church, they were asked to make sworn signed statements to Mennini. But they were also warned that if their complaints became public knowledge, they would cause 'immense further damage to the church'. The church, he says, failed to act quickly and appropriately, adding that he fears the matter was in danger of being swept under the carpet.

He said that the men's complaints were not maliciously motivated. 'I am as sinful as the next man – as my partner and pals frequently remind me. But this isn't about trying to own the moral high ground. I feel compassion for O'Brien, more compassion than the church is showing me, but the truth has to be available – even when that truth is hard to swallow.

A few hours later, on Sunday 3 March, the BBC reported that O'Brien had admitted his sexual misconduct:

In recent days, certain allegations which have been made against me have become public. Initially, their anonymous and non-specific nature led me to contest them.

However, I wish to take this opportunity to admit that there have been times that my sexual conduct has fallen below the standards expected of me as a priest, archbishop and cardinal.

To those I have offended, I apologise and ask forgiveness. To the Catholic Church and people of Scotland, I also apologise.

I will now spend the rest of my life in retirement. I will play no further part in the public life of the Catholic Church in Scotland.

The report went on to say that he would not participate in the conclave to elect the successor of Pope Benedict XVI.

It had been a hard decision to go public. But I believe it was the correct one.

* * *

Pope Francis is a Jesuit, and as such is a follower of Ignation spirituality. Deep within Francis's approach to living out a Christ-like life is the concept of 'discernment'. In a talk he gave to members of the Community of the Pontifical Seminary of Posillipo on Saturday 6 May 2017 in the Vatican's Apostolic Palace he said this:

To become men of discernment, it is then necessary to be courageous, to tell the truth to yourself. Discernment is a choice of courage, contrary to the more comfortable and reductive ways of rigorism and laxism, as I have repeated several times. Educating in discernment means, indeed, fleeing from the temptation to seek refuge behind a rigid norm or behind the image of an idealized freedom. Educating in discernment means 'exposing oneself', coming out of the world of one's own convictions and prejudices to open up to understanding how God is speaking to us, today, in this world, in this time, in this moment, and how He is speaking to me, now.

For our small group, the search for discernment was real, it was hard, and it was not made easier by commentators such as Kearney and Devine (and there were more than the two cited in this book) who felt they just had to explain what was *really* happening in the Church in Scotland at the time.

I felt sad for O'Brien the man. One photo of him at his desk, looking so tired and upset, really hit home. At the end of the day, he was a man in the final phase of his life. He never allowed himself to believe it would end this way. He had been my friend at one point, way in the distant past.

I also felt consumed with the sheer wastefulness of it all.

8

THE POPE'S MEN

Once the story broke in *The Observer*, and with O'Brien now off the centre-stage, it quickly became apparent that the Vatican's position was that the case was now closed. A statement from the Holy See stated that O'Brien 'will be leaving Scotland for a few months for the purpose of spiritual renewal, prayer and penance' (May 2013). But the matter was, in reality, far from settled. I was desperate to know what process the Church would put in place to question basic things like the degree of O'Brien's sexual predation; whether he had behaved criminally; whether he had even opened himself up to blackmail? All these questions, and more, were being left not only unanswered, but unasked, by the Church hierarchy. They did not want to turn over the rock, for fear of what they might find hidden under it.

There was also the question of O'Brien's right to challenge us, his accusers, if he wished to. Due process in every other circumstance would give someone that right. Not, it seems, in the Church.

As the weeks passed, I became increasingly frustrated. Archbishop Philip Tartaglia from Glasgow was appointed administrator of the St Andrews and Edinburgh archdiocese. I knew enough about to him to be confident that he would not help me find the answers I needed. It seemed clear to me that Mennini mishandled the situation badly, so I needed to find someone I could communicate with who had the power to make things happen. Someone whose hand could be forced into action.

Then I remembered the message Fr Mackay had sent us from Rome about our 'courage' – perhaps Cardinal Ouellet, the head of the Congregation for Bishops, would respond. I decided I'd send him a letter. It was hard to tell what the post office clerk was thinking as she processed my registered letter to Vatican City. I was relieved that she couldn't see the contents.

16 March 2013
Dear Cardinal Ouellet,

I would be grateful for your reply to this letter.

On 7th February 2013 I wrote to Archbishop Mennini in London as I was asked to, in order to deliver my sworn statement about the inappropriate actions of Cardinal Keith O'Brien towards me.

Clearly events have moved on and Cardinal O'Brien has admitted his sexual indiscretions and has had his retirement accepted by Pope Emeritus Benedict XVI.

You graciously passed on a message to me and the other original complainants through 'Fr MacKay' thanking us for our courage in making our concerns known.

I have had no official acknowledgement of my complaint having been received and, more importantly, how due process will be followed up by Vatican authorities in relation to Cardinal O'Brien. Archbishop Mennini has not responded to my letter, hence this direct communication to you. I have no desire whatsoever to have Keith O'Brien persecuted. However I do feel that I have a right to know if you intend to have an official, or canonical, inquiry into his actions and behaviour and that he, and perhaps others in positions of power in the Church in Scotland, will be held to account for their practice and poor governance.

Cardinal Ouellet, in this saga much has been said, but I want to know what is being done. I want to know how due process will be pursued and how transparent it will be for me and for other victims of Keith O'Brien's unacceptable behaviour? I am asking this not out of prurience, rather out of a desire to know if the Church will ask real and lasting questions of itself in handling such matters.

You will note in my testimony, which I have appended for your reference, that I decided that I would never be able to be obedient to an Archbishop who was a sexual predator and decided I would rather leave the Priesthood than do so. I also decided not to pursue laicisation because I did not feel my reasons for laicisation would be taken seriously by the Church. I still regard myself as a Catholic . . . albeit a silenced and discarded one. That should demonstrate to you how seriously and deeply I have been affected by Keith O'Brien. And how carefully

I will be observing how the Vatican deals with the Scottish Church and with me.

I look forward to hearing from you.

Sincerely yours,
Anthony Brian Devlin

Ouellet's response? Complete silence.

That thundering silence of the Church is a crushing phenomenon. Many who have suffered abuse and rape by priests comment on the tyrannical silence when they report what they have gone through. Although my pain was a tiny fraction of theirs, I felt the sheer tyrannical weight of the Church pressing down and imagined the most senior leaders thinking, 'Let's just sit this one out' . . . 'Sure, it'll all pass over in good time' . . . 'Hasn't he caused enough scandal for us?'

I was so fed up. I remember sitting one afternoon in my armchair mindlessly watching the television. It was 10 April 2013, almost a month after I sent my letter to Ouellet, and I thought to myself, 'I'm not going to be that person; the one who waits for the letter to drop through the door.' So I decided to phone Ouellet's office just to see what would happen. I looked up the number on Google and rang it.

Never in a month of Sundays did I think he would pick up the phone himself. I had presumed some junior administrator would do things like that. But there he was, the man himself on the end of the line waiting, perplexed, for me to string a coherent sentence together. Eventually I stumbled out my name, where I was calling from and the fact that I was one of the priests who had complained about Keith O'Brien. There was a pause on the line, this time from him, and he asked me who I was again.

I said that I had written to him on 16 March and had had no answer. His response was to ask me if I wanted to discuss this matter over the phone. He didn't know who I was, so I reminded him again that I had written to him and had received no response from him.

He asked if I'd contacted his office, making it clear that he and his department was very busy, and dealt with a lot of issues from around the world. By this time, I could feel the anger and frustration that had been building up inside me over the past few months spill over, as I told this most senior of cardinals in the Vatican that he had better get on with answering my letter.

A few days later, I received a letter with a Congregatio Pro Episcopis stamp on it. Dated 17 April 2013, it read:

> Dear Rev Devlin
> [I wondered at my newly reinstated clerical title]
> I have received your letter of March 16, 2013, with which you also sent me a copy of your letter to the Apostolic Nuncio in Great Britain, Archbishop Antonio Mennini. Thank you for sharing the information with me.
>
> Please know this Dicastery is considering your testimony very carefully. I would ask that you please contact the Apostolic Nuncio in Great Britain for any future needs or concerns.

With assurance of prayers and cordial best wishes,
I remain

Sincerely yours in Christ
Marc Card. Ouellet

So, a cheeky phone call from me had in fact been all it took to unblock the silence. Things began to move at a pace now. On 25 April I received a letter from Mennini apologising for the delay in responding. He offered to 'receive' me if it would be helpful for us to meet. He ended with a jaunty 'With my prayerful good wishes and warm personal regards to you, I remain Yours sincerely in the Lord.'

I was to receive a few of those 'prayerful good wishes' sort of responses over the next while from various high-ranking Church officials. What lay behind those words? They always made me smile. A simple 'Yours sincerely' would have done.

A few days and a couple of phone calls later, a meeting was set up between Mennini and myself. It was to take place in Motherwell in the middle of June 2013. It was to be one of the strangest encounters I've ever participated in in my life.

A few days before the meeting with Mennini was to take place, he appeared on the evening news on the occasion of the announcement of the retiring Bishop of Motherwell, Joe Devine. His comments to the camera were a plea for everyone just to calm down. In his heavily accented statement, Mennini made it clear that he thought O'Brien was, perhaps, being given a bit of a hard time. He said:

'In some aspects, we can also recognise that the cardinal, notwithstanding his mistake, he made a lot of good for the Church. We can't judge the cardinal only for this very serious event because you see in every person there is black and white, the positive, negative and so on.'

In and of itself, there is nothing wrong with Mennini saying what he did. But rather like the Church's press officer, Kearney, the question is, should he have said anything at all? And if he did have to say something could he have, perhaps, thought to say something to bring some sort of comfort for the victims of O'Brien's 'mistake'?

This typical lack of concern by prominent figures in the Church for those who have suffered abuse at the hands of the clergy definitely was profoundly disappointing, and, knowing that I would be meeting Mennini in a few days' time, I realized I had to prepare myself well for this encounter.

I'm rarely late for meetings, and I was an hour early for this one. I waited outside the red-brick church in Motherwell in my car. I was already shattered from the three-hour drive down from the Highlands and I was in very poor health. Doctors had been trying to find out exactly what was wrong with me. Whatever it was, I felt very unwell. The physical pain, as well as the anxiety about the forthcoming meeting, had wiped me out. I'd had nothing to eat for hours and was consumed with nerves. I was, however, determined to make the most of my one shot to meet with this representative of the Pope himself.

I knew exactly what I wanted from the meeting. Simply put, I wanted to know whether the Church had a process to properly investigate our complaints. We had been told that this was a matter only the Pope could resolve. But how was the Pope in Rome going to do this? He could hardly investigate matters himself from Rome.

I was led into the sitting-room of the parochial house, five minutes before the appointed time. White walls and a grey carpet. On one wall was a cheap panoramic view of some cityscape. Its vibrant blue was startling. Underneath was a light-coloured wooden sideboard with two matching table-top lights with wrought-iron stems. In the middle sat a single china bowl. On the other side of the room was a silver-framed television. But my eye was drawn to something next to it which was completely at odds with the setting. It was a model of an aeroplane – the sort you see advertised on in-flight magazines – sitting on a v-shaped stand.

I sat down in one of the armchairs, upholstered in striped fabric. I was mesmerised by this model plane and how out of place it looked. I wondered if any of the priests played with it; lifted it up and made the zooming sound of a jet as they pretended it was flying through the clouds. I was so caught up in these thoughts I was almost surprised when the door opened and in walked Mennini himself, followed by another priest. In too came someone with a plate of sandwiches and some tea and coffee. The priest and the sandwich-bearer left and we were alone. I introduced myself as 'Antonio' (Anthony is my other Christian name) as I've always found Italians tend to mangle 'Brian' into a disconcerting 'Breeann'.

'Antonio. It's good to meet you,' Mennini purred, his accent melodious and friendly. We shook hands.

A tall, slender man, with silvering hair and glasses, he greeted me with full Italian warmth. My eyes were drawn to the thick gold chain he wore around his neck. The pectoral cross that hung from it was tucked away in an inside pocket. I wondered how much it cost? How incongruous it has always seemed to me that members of the Church hierarchy displayed such ostentatious symbols of wealth in a world where so many struggle to survive daily.

He offered me some sandwiches and a drink. I lied to him, claiming I'd eaten previously. I hadn't, of course. I was just concerned that my juddering intestines would melt and liquify.

He had a noble face, and an intense and serious manner. Here is a man, I thought, who is used to getting his own way. So, when he asked if I agreed that the Church had made very significant moves in barring O'Brien from the papal conclave, and sending him off for a period of penance and prayer, it wasn't really a question. It was a statement. I also suspected, as he later confirmed, that he would be reporting back to Cardinal Ouellet in the Vatican, so I felt I had to be very careful with what I said and how I reacted.

I stared directly at him and said that what the Church authorities had done was worthless. Simply hiding O'Brien away had nothing to do with a process which would lead us to truth. Surprisingly, he didn't react. I thought he'd be furious. He wasn't. Or if he was, he was hiding it well.

I explained how important I thought it was for there to be a visible process, where the facts about what O'Brien had actually done could be fully explored. A priest accused of some form of malfeasance would be suspended pending an inquiry, I said, but O'Brien, presumably by dint of being a cardinal, had escaped meaningful scrutiny.

I was just getting into my stride when he asked what sort of process I was looking for. I answered that an ecclesiastical process was what I had in mind. But I did add that perhaps a civil process was not out of question if O'Brien had left himself and therefore the Church open to blackmail due to his sexual predation. He nodded emphatically at that point. He recognised that blackmail was indeed a risk. At this point he leaned forward slightly and murmured quietly that there was a process. It was called an Apostolic Visitation. Now, I'd heard this phrase before. It had happened in Ireland on the back of the reports of wide-scale clerical abuse there. The wind left my sails entirely. This was wholly unexpected. It appeared that Cardinal Ouellet, head of the Congregation for Bishops, had decreed that an investigation would be led by a senior official, and would probe all of the allegations into O'Brien. It was possible that the other priests and I would be involved in this process, and at some point might need to go to Rome to give evidence. I was astonished.

I went on to ask what the likely outcome of such a process would be. Presuming O'Brien was found guilty, I asked if he would be excommunicated (I meant laicised – having his clerical status removed. In the drama of the moment I mixed up my clerical punishments). Mennini's response was intriguing. He seemed to meander in thought for a while, almost thinking out loud. He referred to the case of the notorious Fr Marcial Maciel, a Mexican priest and founder of the Legion of Christ who was proven to have sexually abused a number of boys and young men, to have had sexual relationships with at least two women and to have fathered as many as six children, two of whom he also allegedly abused.

Mennini went on to explain that the Pope had found Maciel guilty but, because of his age, a canonical trial (that is one based on Church law) had been ruled out. Maciel was ordered to 'conduct a reserved life of prayer and penance, renouncing every public ministry'. The same could happen to O'Brien.

I was astounded by what I was hearing: could it be that the process I had wanted was actually going to happen? But then came the rub. Mennini went on to say that the Apostolic Visitation would be led by no less than the soon-to-be appointed new Archbishop of St Andrews and Edinburgh, O'Brien's successor. It was, he declared, an ideal arrangement.

I could feel my blood pressure rising. I suggested that maybe that wasn't a good idea; that there might be a conflict of interest in that arrangement.

This suggestion did not go down at all well.

'Look', I said staring directly at him. 'Let me explain. Can we imagine that you're the new Archbishop, and I'm one of your priests?'

Mennini nodded. It felt odd to be in a role-playing exercise with such a senior cleric.

'You ask me, as part of this process, if I've ever had sex with Cardinal O'Brien.'

He nodded.

'If I had had sex with him, do you think I'd tell you? Of course not,' I continued. 'I'd lie to you.'

His response was to describe what I'd just said as preposterous. Why would anyone lie? 'Precisely because you are the new Archbishop of St Andrews and Edinburgh and I'm going to have to serve under you for years, and you're going to have my entire life in your hands,' I answered.

By this stage I could sense we were both beginning to tire. Mennini spoke a bit about his day. Then we got back to the business in hand. He wanted to know why it was that the other priests and I were only making our complaints known now after so much time. I went over the chronology: how we, the victims, had met up by chance (or perhaps it was God's will) and shared our stories.

He was totally unfazed when I outlined precisely why we had gone public – that the decision to send O'Brien to Rome to lead a life of quiet contemplation had been our breaking point. But he still didn't get it, and couldn't understand why we had taken so long to come forward.

I smiled at him and said, 'Okay, let's imagine you are me and you are a twenty-year old student who has an Irish mamma. Kind of like an Italian mamma, only more so. You want to be a priest and you want to make your mamma proud.'

He nodded.

'Then imagine what happened to me from my spiritual director had happened to you. But let me put it in the context that quite a few of the seminarians and staff in the seminary were homosexual. What do you think would have happened to me and my vocation? That's what I had to deal with.'

He looked genuinely dismayed. He remarked on the gay culture in the Scottish Church. He compared it to *mafiosi*. I was stunned. What an analogy. Well, there sure is an omertà I thought to myself.

By now we were both exhausted. But I had one last point I had to make to him. One that was to make him very angry indeed. I asked him if he'd ever heard of Jimmy Savile? He said yes, he'd heard of him.

'He was a papal knight,' I said. 'A TV personality. Also one of Britain's most notorious paedophiles.' I could tell Mennini wasn't sure where this was heading. I wasn't entirely sure how it would end myself.

'You would never think that it would be a good idea to go on TV and say that while he did some bad things, he also raised vast amounts of money for charity? But that's akin to what you did when you decided to point out, on camera, that despite the fact that he made a mistake, O'Brien did many good things.'

Mennini clearly did not like what he was hearing. He leaned forward and told me that he had chosen every word deliberately. He had, he claimed, received six or seven letters of thanks for what he said from 'normal people' who liked the cardinal very much. There were many out there, he said, who didn't believe what we had been saying.

'I know there are,' I responded. 'That's precisely why we need a process.'

Mennini was now clearly angry. With barely suppressed rage he said he had NOT exonerated the cardinal on television. He repeated that assertion. Finally, he told me with all the authority of the Holy See itself that there was a process, and that if Rome and the Holy Father himself had said there must be an end to this, there would be an end to it. Here was the autocracy and the unflinching self-belief of the Church hierarchy on full display.

It felt as though all the oxygen had left the room. I tried to lighten the mood by changing the subject. I said that I didn't think the Church media office was much good. They'd made things worse. He nodded but told me they were secondary. The process was what was important. It had slipped into the sidelines but was now centre stage again.

As we walked out of the room he told me that he would report back on our meeting to Cardinal Ouellet in the Vatican. He took my hands in his and whilst giving me an Italian embrace he asked for my prayers. 'You are Antonio', he said. 'And I am Antonio too. I like you, Antonio.'

'I like you too, Antonio. But I shall be watching you,' I whispered back.

'Si. Va bene. I have given you my word' he said. And with a promise to visit me in Inverness, our meeting closed.

* * *

Shortly after, I gave *The Observer* an interview outlining what Mennini had said about an Apostolic Visitation, which would be led by the soon-to-be-appointed archbishop.

Experience had told me that engaging with people like Mennini 'off the record' was a dangerous thing to do. On balance it is best to be transparent and open. Neither of us had asked or given any rules about the status of the meeting. I was pretty sure he'd be sharing what had been said with other senior clergy as well as Ouellette back in Rome.

However, after the story of the Apostolic Visitation appeared in print, we drifted into another of those periods of silence. I wrote to Mennini on 5 July 2013, expressing my disappointment that no announcement of the Visitation had yet been made.

His response ten days later appeared curt: 'Any further investigation, as I said, would depend on more evidence and would be the decision of the Archbishop of St Andrews and Edinburgh, who should be named soon.'

So, it looked like the script was being rewritten.

I'm happy now that I threw nothing of relevance away relating to the correspondence around the O'Brien issue, and I have always been a copious note taker around important and key events. I still have a copy of a letter to Pope Francis, written on the 19 July 2013. In it I wrote:

> Cardinal O'Brien has been sent for 6 months' prayer and penance. And then what? Are we expected to regard this as a fair and due process? Indeed, is the cardinal himself not justified to expect [sic] more than this?
>
> Holy Father, I am not asking for much. I simply want to know what is being done, and what will be done, to investigate the abuse and harm caused by Cardinal O'Brien against me and many others.

To this day that letter remains unacknowledged and unanswered.

* * *

In the meantime, a new character appeared blinking into the media glare. Leo Cushley, the new Archbishop of St Andrews and Edinburgh, was appointed. Reports about him said that he had limited pastoral experience but had strong diplomatic credentials. He was regarded as a bright man. I just hoped he had the skills we needed to progress our cause for a just process. He would certainly have a lot of contacts in the Vatican itself. I don't think anyone envied him the job he'd been given.

In an interview with *The Daily Telegraph* on 24 July 2013 he did seem genuinely surprised to find himself sitting in this most uncomfortable of seats:

> Although Mgr Cushley emphasised his lack of pastoral experience for an archbishop's post, he insisted that his postings in some of the world's most troubled regions would mean his new job is 'easy' in comparison.
>
> The Archbishop-elect also promised to drop the incendiary language used by his predecessor in political rows over issues like gay marriage in favour of a more diplomatic and respectful tone.

He seems to have kept his promise about the incendiary language. However, I wonder if in hindsight he regrets describing his new job as 'easy'?

I wrote to him on 21 October 2013 and introduced myself. I sent him a copy of my testimony to Mennini and a plea for him to begin an investigation into matters related to our complaints. The route that had been previously opened up by Mennini at our meeting was now firmly closed down. Cushley really was our only and final hope.

> I now turn to you, Archbishop [I wrote], and ask you to do the right and courageous thing: call for an independent inquiry, root and branch, into the governance of the Archdiocese during Keith O'Brien's charge. It has been reported in the media that the Cardinal had the power to influence the closing down of an audit across Scotland into paedophilia by priests. I want to

be secure, and I am sure that you do too, that such an action can never happen again.

The Cardinal was a predatory man, who took advantage over those who were weaker than he was. He abused not only people, but his position. Are you sure that this abuse would not have left him open to blackmail? Are you sure that the appointments he made were not influenced by his sexual and predatory behaviour? You can't be. No-one can be until an independent investigation into the culture and practice within the Archdiocese and beyond is invoked.

Because he now had my letter outlining what O'Brien had done to me, it would be impossible for Cushley not to agree to meet with me. As the new archbishop he was in charge now. Indeed, to his great credit, he invited all four of the complainants to meet him in his office. The intention was to see us individually. However, we suggested that we'd prefer to see him as a group, though unfortunately one of the priests was unable to attend. He was very accommodating, and a meeting was set up. Having been out of Church circles for so long, and having attended countless boardroom meetings, I knew it was essential that we had to go to that meeting with an agreed set of demands.

It was a cold, dark November night when we met him. The first thing I noticed about him was how shiny his shoes were. He is a tall man, well over six feet, I'd say. He was immaculately dressed in his clerical suit, with the gold chain of his pectoral cross resplendent against his black shirt. He ushered us into his functional office, and we began our discussion. Fr MacKay was present too.

Cushley began by stating that the Holy See – basically the highest of the authorities in the Vatican – had instructed him to be at the disposal of the priests who had made their complaints about O'Brien. It was fascinating to hear Cushley talk. He spoke with the authority that comes with holding high office, even though he was just a few weeks into the job. He knew that we were listening to every word he said, and I waited with bated breath for any information he could give us.

Any canonical judgement, he said, was the prerogative of the Holy See. However, while they were keeping a watching brief on what was going on in the archdiocese and would intervene if matters changed. In essence, though the Vatican's view was 'We're done here'. That was the phrase he used.

As he put it, O'Brien had been punished and humiliated, and unless more evidence was to come forward, no further sanctions or processes would be invoked. Strange word, strange concept, that: humiliated. Did he mean O'Brien was humiliated by his sexual predation being made public? Or was it because he had lost his privileged status? Was his humiliation an end in itself – so there would be no further action?

The next step, Cushley said, was up to us. If we wanted to pursue the case through the courts, then that was our choice. That would be nothing to do with him. He couldn't direct the authorities in Rome because O'Brien was a cardinal.

He'd have been quite happy to show us the door at that point, I suspect, so I asked a quick question. 'What actually went on in the Vatican relating to the handling of O'Brien's case?' On comfortable ground now, he explained that if the case had related to a sexual offence with a minor, it would have been dealt with by the Congregation for the Doctrine of the Faith (CDF). This had been the unit that Joseph Ratzinger ruled with a rod of iron before becoming Pope Benedict XVI. If the case related to 'vulnerable adults', then the concerns would have been dealt with by Cardinal Ouellet and his Congregation for Bishops. He explained that he'd asked an advisor about it all who'd explained: as there was no sin then the matter would go to the Congregation for Bishops. No sin? Clearly my face must have betrayed my thoughts as Fr MacKay quickly intervened, clarifying that there had been sin . . . just not against children.

One of the priests asked why there had been no canonical trial. Cushley thought that was most likely due to O'Brien admitting his guilt. This made sense to me. O'Brien's 'hands up' was clearly a damage limitation exercise, which may well have been imposed on him from on high: a masquerade to avoid the need for a lengthy and more scandal-inducing trial. I pointed out that this was against natural justice and that, not just the accusers, but O'Brien himself had a right to a hearing and, if he chose it, to defend himself.

Cushley nodded. He agreed with this principle but pointed out, once again, that this was a process that was owned by the Holy See. He went on to explain that the nature of the allegations was such that the Congregation for Bishops would have briefed the Pope, who then took the decision to remove O'Brien from the archdiocese, and into prayer and penance in humility. One of us did intervene to point out to Cushley that the initial plan outlined by the Nuncio was not that. Instead it had been to allow

O'Brien to attend the pre-conclave meeting of cardinals, then announce his immediate retirement, after which he might potentially spend the rest of his life in Rome in prayer, like Pope Benedict. That at least had been our fear. Cushley said that he was unaware of that.

It was getting to that stage in a meeting when you're waiting for someone to say 'Well, if there's no further business we'll end it there, shall we?' But we weren't finished yet. It was our turn now. Someone asked about the promise Mennini made about an Apostolic Visitation, with him, Cushley, leading it. No, he said, he had not been asked to do this, but rather to concentrate his efforts on rebuilding the Church. An Apostolic Visitation would be like putting the archdiocese through a shredder, he said, whereas what it needed was tender loving care.

Then we tabled our paper: a paper Cushley knew nothing about prior to the meeting. This had been something I'd prepared earlier and managed to get all of the priests to agree to. I've worked in a large organisation, and I know how other institutions respond to what are called 'adverse incidents'. In my own organisation, Highland Health Board, very high-level mistakes came to light on occasion. My job was to manage the reputation of the organisation, and in particular to work with the media. Our approach to such matters was as far as possible to be one of absolute transparency. This was what I proposed to Cushley in our paper, and it would have been nothing new to anyone who worked in industry or the public sector. It said:

This paper is offered to highlight what we believe are some key areas to be examined in regard to Governance in the Archdiocese. They do not cover the theme of safeguarding which is closely related but is separate.

They are set out around the themes which public organisations would normally follow where there have been 'adverse incidents' or system failures.

Essentially there are three stages in a review of governance where it is established that harm has been caused:

A. A public apology is made to those directly and indirectly affected
B. An analysis is made of how the failure happened in the first place
C. The system is fixed such that lessons are learned and the failure cannot recur.

A PUBLIC APOLOGY

In order to rebuild trust in the governance of the Archdiocese and the Church there needs to be an admission of failure and a public apology to all who have been affected by abusive behaviour and subsequent cover-up. It is not sufficient to point to Cardinal O'Brien as being one bad apple in a barrel. There have been deep rooted systemic and cultural failures across the Catholic Church in Scotland. The media are currently highlighting other failures in governance and it is known in the public domain that several historical cases are being prepared for the Civil Courts.

We would suggest that the apology covers three areas:

- An acknowledgement that wrongdoing has happened, and that harm has been caused to innocent people and a request for forgiveness to follow;
- An acknowledgement that the hierarchy have failed to support the victims adequately and that the time taken to process their complaints has further added to their distress;
- An announcement that an Inquiry will now take place into the governance of the Archdiocese and its remit and findings will be made available to the public.

B. AN ANALYSIS OF WHAT WENT WRONG

Typically, such an analysis should be undertaken by someone with the proper skill set, who is independent and is credible to those who manage the organisation, those who have been affected directly by the event(s), and to the wider Church and society.

We suggest that the following areas may be productive fields of focus for such an analysis:

(a). The process that led to Keith O'Brien being appointed Bishop and then Cardinal.

(b). The extent and degree of Keith O'Brien's sexual predation.

(c). An audit of financial transactions that Keith O'Brien carried out, in order to ensure these were legal, and in keeping with sound financial governance.

(d). Inquiry into whether there was any sacramental abuse by Keith O'Brien, and if there is a possibility of Excommunicatio Latae Sententiae. [This is a very important issue of Church law that I will return to later in this book.]

(e). Whether any appointments or dismissals of priests into or from positions of power or preferential positions could have been made based on failures of good governance by Keith O'Brien.

(f). The role that the members of the Bishops Conference of Scotland have played in allowing Keith O'Brien to block the publication of an audit into paedophilia and abuse by Priests in Scotland without proper challenge.

C. FIXING THE SYSTEM

This third part is the most difficult to address at this stage. It is not possible to prescribe corrective strategies and set up new structures until the diagnostic analysis has been completed. A key element has to be to ensure no one ever again has the latitude to be able to be so unaccountable in their governance.

We believe that successful completion of the first two stages will provide both a positive framework and foundation to rebuild trust in the Church in Scotland and could be seminal in providing a 'reboot' of the faith community that has been so badly hurt and let down by events.

The paper concluded with some points about a statement from the Scottish bishops about safeguarding. There was nothing threatening, nothing frightening, and nothing particularly new in it. This is just standard stuff for any organisation to take on board when it deals with crisis or reputation management. We just applied it to the Church.

Cushley read the paper in complete silence. The meeting he had planned had been taken in another direction. There began a lengthy discussion about an apology, the nature of an apology, and who it was that should do the apologising. In other words, a typical circular clerical discussion that goes on and on without reaching a conclusion. So, finally, I asked Cushley to give me one satisfactory and rational reason why the Church wouldn't apologise to O'Brien's victims. Significantly, he asked for time to reflect and take further advice on the matter. He agreed that an apology, such as that outlined, *could* be made, but he had to seek advice on what would be the best choice of action.

We then moved on to the other governance issues the paper referred to: feelings of deep unease at the appointment of one of O'Brien's intimate circle of friends to a highly significant position.

Whilst preparing for the meeting I had been reading some correspondence exchanged with the archdiocese and I noticed that it was registered as a Scottish charity. A quick check on Google and it was confirmed. It is a multi-million-pound business. As such the archdiocese was under the governance of the law of the land. Along with the benefits of charitable status come the responsibilities of ensuring that proper governance issues were in place now, and had been in place, when O'Brien was in charge. The Charity Regulator takes all of these matters seriously, I pointed out. A tired

Cushley agreed. It seemed clear to me he wanted us out now.

There was much in our paper that he thought he could take forward. But he would need to consult his advisors and superiors as to what he would be allowed to do.

By the end of the meeting there was only me and another priest left (the third member of our party had had to leave early to conduct a service). We walked out in silence together. I felt unable to breathe until we got into his car. All in all, it seemed to have gone rather well. I was elated.

9

THERE CAN BE NO OMERTÀ

Four months after our meeting with Cushley, the Holy See's 'We're done here' was thrown in the bin. An official letter was sent to every priest in the archdiocese. It intoned in that peculiar voice that the Church uses when it demands that you sit up and listen, as it has something very important to say:

> *AD CLERUM*
>
> Acting upon the request of His Holiness Pope Francis, the Congregation for Bishops has mandated and authorised the Right Reverend Charles Scicluna, Auxiliary Bishop of Malta, to listen to and report the testimony offered by past and present members of the clergy of the Archdiocese of St Andrews & Edinburgh concerning any incidents of sexual misconduct committed against them by other members of the clergy whomsoever.
>
> Anyone who has suffered such misconduct and who wishes to advise the Holy See of his experience is invited to come forward at this time.
>
> Bishop Scicluna will be available to listen to you on Tuesday 8, Wednesday 9 and Thursday 10 April 2014.

In order to facilitate the hearings, Bishop Scicluna has asked that those who intend to approach him prepare their narrative in writing.'

It finished with details where any past and present members of the clergy should make contact.

It was signed Leo Cushley.

The overwhelming emotion I had was one of sheer relief. We had forced this hard, unyielding superstructure to listen to us and to change its course. The last thing the Church wanted to happen had now come to pass, and it was right that it did. This had moved way beyond O'Brien. This was now about the governance of the Church. It was also a lesson in the values of perseverance. It came at a terrible cost of energy, time and effort. My health had deteriorated badly, but my immediate concern was that I would find it difficult to make the trip to Edinburgh to meet with Bishop Scicluna.

No need. Scicluna, I was told, would travel north to meet me at my house. In fact, Leo Cushley offered to drive him. Practicalities, however, eventually meant that in the end, he couldn't, and another priest was appointed as Scicluna's chauffeur for the day. Out of the three days he was to spend in Scotland, the major part of one of them was with me in the Highlands.

The Church authorities could not have behaved better. It's true that they had not done so without being forced – but they did, eventually, do the right thing. This was exactly the Church that I wanted to meet, that I wanted to hear from. It cost them nothing, and it gained them a great deal of respect from me.

But first, who is Bishop Charles Scicluna?

Put simply, he is one of the most courageous and outspoken pursuers of truth and justice in the Catholic Church, especially in the area of child sex-abuse by the clergy. Along the way he will undoubtedly have made enemies within the ecclesiastical establishment, but his eye has always been on the prize: a Church, free from abuse, that can claim to be the embodiment of Christ's ministry on earth.

As I read about Scicluna, one thing in particular impressed itself on me. It was a moment when the past and the present crashed into one another. On 21 June 2012 the *National Catholic Reporter* published an article by Jason Berry on the huge scandal that had engulfed the Vatican during the reign of Pope John Paul II. It concerned the Fr Marcial Maciel, the same priest Mennini referred to in my meeting with him and who he was paralleling O'Brien's likely fate with. The article included this short paragraph outlining a crucial role Scicluna had played:

> A picture is emerging of Maciel's deceptions and the order's disinformation campaign in defending him as enmeshed with key figures in the Roman Curia, as well as the past and present Popes. The Legion has been in a revolving door of investigations under the Congregation for the Doctrine of the Faith since 2004, when then Cardinal Joseph Ratzinger ordered an investigation by canon lawyer Msgr. Charles Scicluna. Scicluna traveled to America and Mexico, taking dozens of testimonies by Maciel's sexual victims for the report he delivered after Ratzinger became Pope. Since 2010, the Vatican has held the Legion in a receivership, with a

continuing inquiry of the Legion's lay wing, Regnum Christi. But Vatican oversight has been timid, yielding cosmetic changes amid a swamp of Legion scandals rooted in the tactics of psychological coercion put in place by Maciel to shield his secret life, money for his morphine addiction, and to support four out-of-wedlock children by two women.

If ever a story has pointed to how deeply Catholicism's well has been contaminated, then it is this one. And here was Scicluna coming to Scotland to investigate the complaints made against O'Brien.

Since the work he did in Scotland, Scicluna's stardom has been on the rise. He has been made Archbishop of Malta, appointed as Adjunct Secretary for the Congregation of the Doctrine of the Faith and he has been the Pope's lieutenant in the handling of serious and sensitive cases of sex abuse involving senior Church figures. This was evidenced when Pope Francis made a catastrophic error of judgement over complaints about a bishop in Chile who, it was alleged, covered up sexual abuse of children by a prominent and charismatic priest.

Pope Francis sent Scicluna along with Fr Jordi Bertomeu Farnós to listen to the testimonies of the victims. On 20 March 2018 they in turn presented the Pope with their report. As a direct consequence of this, at a meeting between Francis and Chile's bishops, all of the bishops offered their resignations.

If there had been any remaining doubt that the Church would not be taking the charges against O'Brien with the utmost seriousness, then that was dispelled with the appointment of Scicluna. A friend sent me a paper Scicluna had written called 'The Quest for Truth in Sexual Abuse Cases: A Moral and Legal Duty'. In it he said, 'the teaching of Blessed John Paul II that truth is the basis of justice explains why a deadly culture of silence or 'omertà' is in itself wrong and unjust'. The mafia language was startling once again.

* * *

Margaret Mary, my wife, and I, believe that offering hospitality is a gift. However, when I saw the groaning table of food that she'd prepared for Scicluna and his driver, I thought she'd overdone it. Two different pots of soup on the go; plates of quiche; platters of various cheeses; a basket of mixed breads; mounds of fruit. Water, still and sparkling. Teas: green, herbal, Earl Grey, Lady Grey and Typhoo. 'It's not the Borgias who are coming, is it?' I asked her.

The car slipped quietly into our drive and Margaret Mary and I both went out to meet our guests. Out of the car came a diminutive, immaculate man. He was stiff from the long journey up the A9 and I noticed him wince as he pulled himself slowly out of his seat. We were both talking to his driver, a priest who had noticed our rare breed hens, since he was a chicken fancier himself. But my eye was drawn to Scicluna. He meticulously put on his black raincoat over his equally black clerical suit, put his beret on his head, gathered his bag and together we walked the twenty yards to our front door where he removed them all again with the same meticulous concentration. Luckily, Margaret Mary had cleaned the path of chicken poo and the hens were moaning their frustration at being corralled in their runs, unable to forage for the worms and seeds as they were used to doing.

We live in a spectacular area of Scotland and Scicluna murmured in appreciation at our view which towers over the Moray Firth and the battlements of Fort George. He took his phone out and started taking photos.

We sat in our small sunroom. Margaret Mary and the chauffeur priest were talking chicken-talk in one corner, and I sat next to Scicluna. He'd only recently been promoted to the rank of bishop. 'Do you like being a bishop?' I asked.

He smiled. He loved being a bishop. He loved being able to preach to so many people. His melodic voice was engaging. He told me that he had read the dossier I'd prepared for him, on the journey north. 'There's really one question I want to ask you,' he said to me quietly. 'It's about your identity.'

'Of course,' I said. 'Would you like something to eat and then we'll get started?'

I stayed where I was whilst the others went off to get something to eat. My mind though was in a spin. My identity? My identity? What did that mean? Was he thinking maybe my *sexual* identity? I was internalising an anxiety attack that was distorting and overblowing things. They all wandered back in with plates of soup.

All the while Scicluna ate his soup serenely. He looked out at the display of daffodils swaying in the garden. He explained a connection between St David and daffodils. 'St David's Day is the anniversary of my ordination,' I said. He finished his soup. Right, I thought, let's get cracking.

He followed me slowly to the kitchen 'Would you like some

quiche?' Margaret Mary asked. 'Say no!' I screamed inwardly. 'I want to know why he's asking about my identity!'

Scicluna asked me why I wasn't eating. I explained that my health was bad. We walked back to the sunroom. Everyone else ate happily, commenting on the view. And the chickens. He finished his quiche. 'Cheese?' my wife asked. Oh, for the love of God!

He folded his napkin tidily as he finished. 'Would you like some fruit?' Margaret Mary asked.

'Why don't we take the fruit and a cup of tea with us and we can get started?' I suggested. We settled ourselves in the living room. He sat on my late father's green upright leather chair and we talked.

In turned out there was, after all, nothing sinister in his question about my identity. He said that he would have to talk to O'Brien as part of the process. The opening paragraph to the Nuncio, in my letter, said that my identity had to remain anonymous and could not be shared without my express permission. I was so moved by that simple thought. Here he was asking my permission to mention me if he needed to. By now I was so used to liberties being taken, with little regard for my welfare, by bishops and priests and armchair Catholic commentators, I was moved by the manner of this civilised man.

We talked about the whole panoply of my story. Softly he said that he felt sorry for my 'mamma'. A cleaner and home-help. Someone who wanted the best for her son. Someone who worked so hard. We talked about O'Brien; about what he'd actually done to me. I was amazed when he said that he felt that O'Brien's bedside apology to me the morning after he had abused me was indicative that he'd done that sort of thing before.

He looked across at me sincerely as he said this and the emotion welled up. Here, finally, was someone who believed me.

We talked about what I did after I'd left the priesthood and I told him of working with heroin users; with people with AIDS; with women caught up in prostitution. Lost and lonely people. That was when he suggested that whilst I had left the priesthood, I had continued to be true to my vocation and had never really stopped ministering to people; I had just been doing so in a different way.

Turning to practical matters, he explained that the Pope had mandated him to collect all of the evidence that he could, and present a report of the situation surrounding O'Brien and the archdiocese. It was then, he said, in the hands of Pope Francis. 'What do you think he'll do?' I asked.

He really had no idea. A new Pope, new style. It was impossible to predict.

As Scicluna departed I felt that I had met someone very special indeed; someone who was fearless in pursuit of justice, and a genuinely honourable man. For the first time, I felt that the emotions and fears I'd handed over to someone would be cared for and respected.

We waved him off, went inside and closed the door.

Then, apart from one further encounter with Scicluna, there was complete radio silence from Church authorities.

* * *

On March 20th, 2015, just short of a year since Bishop Scicluna began his investigation, the Vatican made the following announcement in Italian and in English:

Comunicato stampa del Decano del Collegio Cardinalizio, 20.03.2015

The Holy Father has accepted the resignation of the rights and privileges of a Cardinal, expressed in canons 349, 353 and 356 of the Code of Canon Law, presented by His Eminence Cardinal Keith Michael Patrick O'Brien, Archbishop Emeritus of Saint Andrews and Edinburgh, after a long period of prayer. With this provision, His Holiness would like to manifest his pastoral solicitude to all the faithful of the Church in Scotland and to encourage them to continue with hope the path of renewal and reconciliation.

This meant that, whilst retaining the title of cardinal, O'Brien's glass was now empty. He could take no part in further ministry in the Church. He could play no further role in the College of Cardinals in future conclaves. He got to keep his title and his red hat. But he could only wear it within the privacy of his own home.

The BBC News carried the final statement from O'Brien himself:
I wish to repeat the apology which I made to the Catholic Church and the people of Scotland some two years ago now on 3 March 2013.

I then said that there have been times that my sexual conduct has fallen below the standards expected of me. For that, I am deeply sorry.

I thank Pope Francis for his fatherly care of me and of those I have offended in any way.

I will continue to play no part in the public life of the Church in Scotland; and will dedicate the rest of my life in retirement, praying especially for the Archdiocese of St Andrews and Edinburgh, for Scotland, and for those I have offended in any way'.

Cushley's own statement in the BBC report was more curt:

Cardinal O'Brien's behaviour distressed many, demoralised faithful Catholics, and made the Church less credible to those who are not Catholic.

I therefore acknowledge and welcome his apology to those affected by his behaviour and also to the people of Scotland, especially the Catholic community.

For my own part, I would like to express sorrow and regret to those most distressed by the actions of my predecessor.

I also pay tribute to those who had the courage to come forward to speak to Archbishop Scicluna.

I hope now that all of us affected by this sad and regrettable episode will embrace a spirit of forgiveness, the only spirit that can heal any bitterness and hurt that still remains.

I read the word 'courage' once more, and wondered once again at what was really meant by it. I found out about this announcement through Twitter. There was no personal communication from the Church authorities in Scotland or in Rome. I was not offered sight of Scicluna's report, not even a redacted version of it. It may be that it never crossed anyone's mind that I would have a desire or even the right to see what had been written about me.

In his statement, O'Brien made reference to the 'fatherly care' Pope Francis had given both him 'and those I have offended in any way'. I'm still waiting to be offered some of that care, fatherly or otherwise, from this most pastoral of popes. I don't suppose I'll hear from him anytime soon.

What I have felt, though, during this very long and tiring journey is the care of people who do love me. Their friendship and warmth has comforted me. This is what us lay people must do as an authentic Church. We must care for one another as Jesus told us to do, not as the hierarchy of the Church pretend to.

PART TWO

WHERE DO WE GO? HOW DO WE HEAL?

10

SEEKING REDEMPTION FOR A BROKEN CHURCH

That, then, is the Life of Brian. Or part of it. What I want to do now, as an aging man should, is tell you what I make of it all.

But first I need to be honest with you. Here is how I feel about being a Catholic much of the time. The wonderful Irish writer Maeve Binchy described herself as a 'collapsed Catholic'. I read this a while ago and have applied it to myself ever since. It's even in my Twitter profile.

At times I reflect on O'Brien and Drygrange and the travails of the Church, and I groan. I collapse inwardly and say, 'I can't be bothered anymore.'

I hear the tale of some priest asking his parishioners for donations of thousands of pounds for new vestments for his liturgical parades and I groan again.

I am collapsed. But I am Catholic. My interest is observational on a level. I don't go to church often, and I don't receive the sacraments as a true Catholic should. When I am admitted to hospital and asked my religion I say 'none' because I don't want, nor need, a priest at my bedside. If

I travel to Rome it's for the pasta and the paintings, not for the prayer.

But being a collapsed Catholic does not mean I have rejected the Church in which I was brought up, and which I tried to serve in my younger years. In fact, I feel it gives me a unique perspective to view the problems the Church faces, and is a larger, and more liberating, 'call to serve'. It is, however, a call that requires inner resources and the stamina to stick with it.

A Church of Frailties

In the introduction to this book I asked this question: 'why do low standards of behaviour, scandal and abuse continue to happen with such regularity in the Catholic Church and, when they do, why does it matter to people so much?'

It's only fair that I attempt to construct some sort of a reflection to address that question before I go on to offer some specific recommendations for reform.

I feel, looking back on my own life, that I have been blessed and enhanced by having had the opportunity to be a priest. I was given an opportunity that few have, to come close to people and walk beside them when they were heavily burdened. Priesthood has given me tools and sensitivities that have shaped and moulded me. More than anything, it has given me the courage to stand up against those in 'power' when I have felt and suspected injustice.

I have a theory, based on experience, that big organisations– and I don't know if there is any bigger than the Catholic Church – all act broadly similarly when they are challenged about the behaviour of their leaders.

We have seen, up close and personal, how the Church behaved over the whistleblowing about O'Brien. There were threats, denial, anger, sullen silence and, eventually, acceptance that the matter needs to be investigated by someone independent of the immediate structure. Still a cleric, sure. But a trusted one.

In one of those strange occurrences in life, as I have been writing this book I have been working voluntarily on another project. One of the most fascinating exercises I've ever undertaken in my professional life.

My career in the health service ended abruptly due to ill health that had been brought on through abusive bullying in my workplace. My bully took to dismantling me in private and in public (Up until then I'd had little but support, appreciation and positive feedback from my employers). It reached a point where I became very unwell indeed. I survived, just, and with hard work and over time I healed.

So, when I was approached ten years later by a group of whistleblowers – four doctors who felt that the culture of NHS Highland where I had worked was contaminated by bullying – to ask if I would help them with the media management of their campaign, I lost no sleep over agreeing to support them.

Like the priests with O'Brien, the whistleblowers in the health organisation went to the media having exhausted every possible internal mechanism to get the powers that be to take their concerns seriously. Every avenue had been blocked. Every time they had tried to engage in discussion they were thwarted. Just as the priests and I went to the Papal Nuncio, the doctors navigated the committee structures of the health board. To no avail.

When the nuclear option was chosen – to go public through the media – the reactions of the health organisation and the Church were mirror images of one another. Outrage. Denial. The whistleblowers were not to be trusted. There was no problem. It was all just gossip. As our media campaign ratcheted up, more and more people came forward. It was a sobering time for the health service. Anger gave way to consternation. Outrage softened to a desire to talk, to understand.

Gradually, at a glacial pace, there was a recognition that there was indeed a problem. But would facing up to that problem cause further 'scandal'? Would the organisation's reputation be irrevocably damaged?

Eventually, showing remarkable personal and political courage, the Minister for Health for Scotland, Jeane Freeman, commissioned an independent inquiry by a senior law officer which did, in fact, recognise that very real and lasting harm and injury had been caused. As in the O'Brien case, the NHS Highland bullying story is worth pondering and learning lessons from.

So, my first reflection on my question about why things go wrong is a simple one. They go wrong because organisations are run by humans. And humans are flawed. Both the Church and the health organisation were failed by those in positions of leadership. It wasn't the laity that poisoned the Catholic Church. It was the bishops, and cardinals. In the health organisation it wasn't the patients or the frontline staff who corrupted the culture. It was the leadership.

I detect another similarity between the two.

I have a natural affinity for whistleblowers. Of course, having been one myself, you'd expect me to say that. There's something about the makeup, the ethical profile of whistle-blowers, that intrigues me. They are highly attuned to the welfare of others. They are sympathetic creatures who care when things go wrong, and seek to make the best possible decision that they can. The whistleblowers I know found the courage to do what they did because they trusted one another. They are 'sinners' with weaknesses and flaws, yet they strive to attain the highest level of 'good' behaviour. They are diligent. They do not cut corners. They understand the power of detail.

These characteristics all form the basis for a well-known and respected approach to ethics, called Virtue Ethics. It is spoken of widely in moral theological circles. The key text on this is found in the seminal book *Principles of Biomedical Ethics* by Tom Beauchamp and James Childress, in which the authors define five 'focal' virtues: compassion, discernment, trustworthiness, integrity and conscientiousness (Chapter two, 8th edition 2019).

Whistleblowers will always be a part of the landscape in all organisations. They need to be. They are the reminder we need that, in our flawed state, things will always go wrong and lessons must always be learned. And sometimes that means speaking up in public.

My analogy between the health board and the Church may be more or less insightful, but it is limited in at least one solemn regard. The health board does not claim divine inspiration.

That's why it matters deeply when things go wrong, as they have done with such devastation in the Catholic Church. I'll delve into this in a bit more depth further on. But

I want to talk about one specific aspect that I believe Catholics need to be woken up to. I call it 'the hoax of leadership'.

I think most right-thinking people, within and outside Catholicism, would say that the Church is both deeply obsessed and deeply mistaken in its sexual ethics. Without going into too much of the theological packaging of Church teaching on sex, the main premise, based on a notion called Natural Law, is that sex is focused on the procreation of children.

Because of the psychological and spiritual dominance that the Church has over its followers, this self-belief of the 'one, holy, catholic and apostolic', is regarded as normative. Were it say to come from a sect like The Branch Davidians in Waco Texas, the response would be different, to say the least.

But let's delve into this a bit more. How far from acceptable does the hoax of leadership take us when we consider sex?

In 'Love and Responsibility' by Karol Wojtyla (later Saint Pope John Paul II) we find a passage in chapter five about 'medical sexology'. This particular '-ology' 'seeks to regulate man's actions in the interest of his health'. My attention to this passage was raised by Catholic academic and former President of Ireland Mary McAleese, who was making a presentation in Dublin where she quoted from this section: 'sexual intercourse, the sexual act between a woman and a man, is unthinkable without an act of Will, especially on the part of the man.'

John Paul II continues:

> It is in the very nature of the act that the man plays the active role and takes the initiative, while the woman is a comparatively passive partner, whose function

it is to accept and to experience. For the purposes of the sexual act it is enough for her to be passive and unresisting, so much so that it may even take place without her volition while she is in a state in which she has no awareness at all of what is happening – for instance while she is asleep or unconscious. In this sense intercourse depends on the man's decision.

Is the Pope condoning rape within marriage? It's hard to say. He uses the word 'volition' and not consent. He doesn't say a man *should* have sexual intercourse with a sleeping or unconscious woman. Just that he *could* – if he wanted to. (He follows up his thoughts by saying that this is within the context which 'excludes exploitation of the person'.)

But the real question is: who so forensically ploughs into detailed analysis of sexual intercourse in such a way? The answer is men – old men who promise not to have sex. Worse still, the faithful are expected to agree with and accept such sage advice. This epitomises why things go so badly wrong in the Catholic Church, and why it matters when they do. It's because the leaders don't understand the world we live in, and in this case, they have turned the teaching on the ethics of sexual intercourse into an instruction manual akin to one that explains the workings of a carburettor. Even a cursory look at the teachings of Aristotle, from which the theory of natural law and all Catholic ethics emanates, demonstrates his belief that ethical knowledge is not mere abstract theory, but rather that a person must gain it from 'experience of the actions in life'.

This fascination about sex and its close cousin, sin, has been part of the Christian story since its initiation. In Peter

Brown's *The Body and Society: Men, Women and Sexual Renunciation in Early Christianity*, we read (p. 140) that

> Pagan conviction that Christians met in order to indulge in sexual promiscuity died hard. This was hardly surprising: by the year 200, every Christian group had accused its own Christian rivals of bizarre sexual practices. In the time of Justin, a young man in Alexandria even petitioned the Augusta Prefect for permission to have himself castrated. Only by undergoing this drastic operation could he hope to persuade pagans that indiscriminate intercourse was not what Christian men sought in their 'sisters'.

But it was St Augustine who most famously interpreted the Genesis story, writes Brown (p. 399), as meaning that:

> ...sexuality, hence marriage and the creation of the family, could only have followed the Fall of Adam and Eve. They were the result of a sad decline, by which Adam and Eve, had lapsed from an "angelic" state into physicality, and so into death. A question mark was allowed to hover over human society. Marriage, and the structures that sprang from it, could not be derived from the original nature of the human person. Ascetic exegesis of the Fall of Adam and Eve tended to preserve, at the back of the minds of its exponents, a lingering doubt: society, marriage, and, if not those, certainly sexual intercourse, were fundamentally alien to the original definition of humanity.

Sex is and always has been a messy business for Catholicism. This tie-in with sin and less than perfection is grist to the mill for the Church. It lies deep in the DNA. And its power is corrosive. Although, undoubtedly, they would deny it, the hierarchy hold onto a deep-set belief that their celibacy raises them above those in sexually committed relationships. However, things are never straightforward.

Christopher Caldwell writes in *The New York Times* international edition (February 26, 2020) that:

> when society turned liberationist, as it did in the 1960's and '70s, hidden sexualities emerged. The church had become a nest of difficult-to-socialise libidos, and a vast number of priestly molestation cases followed, peaking between 1970 and 1980. The rocky transition into sexual modernity has done lasting damage to the church's reputation, especially when it comes to its teachings concerning sexuality.

The hierarchy of Catholicism rails against the tide of secularism and permissiveness of society; of the cheapening of sex. Yet they themselves cheapen it further by their words, their analyses, and their teachings. They have no right, no destiny, to speak authoritatively about sex because, in this, as in many matters of ethics, they do not know the full picture. They have no more right to speak authoritatively about sex than I do to speak authoritatively about the art collections in the Vatican museum. I might admire them from afar. I might even comment on their appeal. But I'd never claim specialist knowledge and never put myself in the position of telling others what their nuances are. Insofar as these celibate old men claim they do indeed have authority, then their claim is a hoax. It is dangerous, and those who follow it without criticism are part of the problem that the Church has.

To sum up then, it is entirely possible to think of the Church as 'one, holy, Catholic and apostolic' institution, while at the same time recognise it as flawed because it is run by humans. But perhaps 'flawed' is too soft a term to describe the horrors that the clerical abuse scandals have demonstrated. As horror stories crash to the shore, day after day, month after month, and the pain and suffering that has been so cruelly meted out to innocent victims, the Church, which should be pulsating with shame and humility, instead has responded with anger, denial, callousness and often silence. But more and more people, men, who thought themselves to be above the law, are being pulled before civic society as criminals and treated with the exacting fairness of society's justice instead of the self-serving, longstanding tenets of canon law regarding abuse.

The hoax of leadership within the Church, this mirage of authority that allows old men who have never had sex to speak with such graphic intensity about this or that 'sex act' as though they have any role whatsoever in the intimate lives of Catholics, is bizarre. It's the language and behaviour of a cult where common sense is left at the door.

With all that being said, it is important to seek solutions and not just mumble in the corner about how woeful everything is.

The following reflections are based on my experiences and thoughts that I first considered in my years in Drygrange. But in the intervening years they have been brought into clearer focus following the events I've recounted in this book.

These are not spiritual reflections – rather they focus on structure and governance; the role of women in ministry as a civil rights issue; the abuse of power and a misplaced and hypocritical sexual ethic; an approach to sin as an accounting practice and the concept of 'scandal' that tends to generate cover up of malfeasance in the Church. They are largely structural and theological reflections and none of them are beyond embrace. In fact, none of them are even original. Each of them would, I believe, offer a partial solution to the current problems of the Church.

Whose Church is it Anyway?

If you had to describe the structure of the Catholic Church to a passing alien, what image would you chose? The one that most readily springs to my mind is a pyramid. The man dressed in white, the pope, sits at the top. He's the emperor. All emperors have a court and, of course, an empire.

Below him there are rows and rows of brightly coloured dignitaries. Dressed in red are the cardinals. The pope is picked from that group. Then come various ranks of arch-bishops, bishops, right down to the men and women in religious orders and priests. By and large these 'promoted' people are well up in years. The court is shrinking.

Let's put some numbers next to them to get a sense of the size of the court. Helpfully, the Vatican produces statistics now and again on these things. The latest are taken from 20 October 2018. Worldwide there are 5,353 bishops and 414,969 priests. (It's arguable whether priests really make up the court. Most of them won't even have had lunch with the top brass.)

There are just over 200 cardinals. There is obviously just the one pope. So, when you set these figures against the 1.299 billion population of Catholics in the world the court is relatively small. But it is hugely powerful. It steers one of the largest global organisations on the planet. Despite the existence of 659,445 women religious throughout the world, the court is exclusively male.

There is no denying the enormity of Catholicism and its power and influence. It is a structure that has its advantages. There are very clear lines of authority. We all know who the boss is. It is an organisation that does not like dissent, and so people who are unhappy with the rules have no alternative but to leave, though that is not such an easy thing to do.

It has lasted for 2,000 years and it has a long organisational memory. And, of course, as we know, by its own creed, it is the 'one, holy, catholic and apostolic' Church. These four 'marks' of the Church lead it to regard itself as holding a position of supreme importance as a route of the Divine. The succession of its bishops, right back to the apostles themselves, allows the Church to speak with firm authority that what it teaches reflects the will of God.

However, this is a structure which, if corrupted, means that the entire edifice risks becoming tainted, hence compromising God's word. Since we cannot doubt the very real power of Catholicism, neither can we deny the systemic corruption that has befallen it. The headlines and stories are without end; of sexual cruelty to children and adults by members of the clergy; of bishops who, somehow, developed a way of thinking where they gathered that it would be better to cover up rather than expose the horrifying behaviour of some of their priests; of cardinals, a few footsteps from the pope, shamed because of their actions; of abuse victims in agony not only as a result of being the object of someone else's cruelty; but also because the Church tries too often to silence their voices and to protect the perpetrators.

The priests, bishops and religious who are trying their best to live within their vows and vocations are damaged because they see the pain inflicted upon the innocent, and many are unfairly and unjustifiably tarred with the same brush as those who have been found guilty the most horrific abuse.

The laity look on in sheer desperation as they hear and see the horrifying tales of what has happened to their neighbours, their daughters and sons, and their fellow parishioners. They are left devastated and questioning the very basis of their faith.

The well that Catholics have drunk from has become poisoned. And, sadly, the poison has largely emanated from within the court of the emperor. This colossal organisation, known throughout the world for good work, heroic achievement and sacrifice is now firmly associated with the most hideous crimes, and the cowardly and cynical attempts of its leadership to cover them up. Keith O'Brien was a rank amateur when it comes to some of the abusers whose stories have been reported, but he is indicative of the rot nonetheless. So where can the Church go from here? How can we heal? How do we re-find Catholicism? My proposal is that we re-examine how the Church operates. In fact we are already allowed to do that. The Pope told us so.

The Second Vatican Council was instituted by Pope John XXIII in 1962. It was a gathering of Church leaders and theologians from across the Catholic world to upgrade the Church's teachings on a range of doctrines. It concluded in 1965 and produced a range of, in Catholic terms, ground-breaking documents that have governed the teachings of the Church ever since. Famously, it allowed Mass and liturgical services to be modernised and removed the necessity for them to be held in Latin. But it was much more than that.

I'm not a great one for reading papal speeches. They have a tone and language that thunders, but this short bit of text is worth a look. In his opening address to the Council, the Pope outlined the fundamentals of its teaching authority:

> The substance of the ancient doctrine of the deposit of faith is one thing, and the way in which it is presented is another. And it is the latter that must be taken into great consideration with patience if necessary, everything being measured in the forms and proportions of a magisterium which is predominantly pastoral in character.

The 'magisterium' referred to is the official teaching office of the Church. So, the 'substance', the guts, of the faith doesn't change – but how it is presented can. An important document created by the Council that is relevant to this discussion is called *Lumen Gentium* (Light of the Nations). As well as being astonishing in its power, *Lumen Gentium* holds within it one of the most profound teachings in Catholicism. It prompts us to reflect on the question: 'Whose Church is it?', which is to be found in Chapter 4, section 35 – where the concept of *Sensus Fidelium* (The Sense of the Faithful) is outlined. It's heavy stuff, but essentially what it says is that lay people have a divine gift whereby they can, together with the ecclesiastical hierarchy, understand and interpret faith. Arguably that interpretation is seen very evidently in the 'faithful' rejecting the Church's teaching on artificial contraception (by a margin of 95 per cent some surveys indicate). Not many large families nowadays fill the pews, but I imagine just as much sexual intercourse is occurring. Evidencing, perhaps, the astute recognition by the laity that, whilst they do have a role in the Church's boardrooms, the Church has no right of presence in the bedrooms of the faithful.

This teaching on *Sensus Fidelium* is significant. It is telling us something very fundamental. It is teaching us that, whilst the hierarchy have their role in discerning God's will, it is a distinct but no more important role than the laity has. In other words, the Church belongs to all the people of God, not exclusively to the clergy.

On a similar theme, 'synodality' is a concept often quoted by Pope Francis, who became Pope in 2013. *The National Catholic Reporter*, a very influential Catholic newspaper in the United States, outlined on 4 May 2018 the importance given to the inclusion of lay people in the authority structures of the Church. The story referred to a report, which was approved by the Pope, indicating that such involvement is 'indispensable': 'The participation of lay faithful is essential . . . They are the immense majority of the People of God and we have much to learn from their participation in diverse expressions of life.'

Throughout the centuries, the laity have been led to believe that the Church really should be run by priests, bishops and popes. They have often been made to feel that they are the lesser members of the Church. This is a distorted view.

How best to describe a truer role for lay people in Catholicism?

I'm an Irish-Scot so the word I use is 'minding'. It's a word used a lot in our Celtic conversations. We're told to 'mind ourselves', meaning we have to be attentive to our situation and the dangers we might be in. We might be charged to 'mind the bairn' – to keep the baby of the house safe from harm – and the old Highland farmer might wonder who is going to 'mind the farm' after he dies. The laity have a role in minding the Church: of being guardians of its true and fundamental nature, minding the very way of living that Jesus espoused in the Beatitudes from the Sermon on the Mount.

> Seeing the crowds, he went onto the mountain. And, when he was seated, his disciples came to him.
> Then he began to speak. This is what he taught them:
> How blessed are the poor in spirit: the kingdom of Heaven is theirs.
> Blessed are the gentle: they shall have the earth as inheritance.
> Blessed are those who mourn: they shall be comforted.
> Blessed are those who hunger and thirst for uprightness: they shall have their fill.
> Blessed are the merciful: they shall have mercy shown them.

Blessed are the pure in heart: they shall see God.

Blessed are the peacemakers: they shall be recognised as children of God.

Blessed are those who are persecuted in the cause of uprightness: the kingdom of Heaven is theirs.

Blessed are you when people abuse you and persecute you and speak all kinds of calumny against you falsely on my account.

Rejoice and be glad, for your reward will be great in heaven; this is how they persecuted the prophets before you.

You are salt for the earth. But if salt loses its taste, what can make it salty again? It is good for nothing, and can only be thrown out to be trampled under people's feet.'

(The New Jerusalem Bible Reader's Edition,
Matthew 5:2–13)

These are the values that Jesus left us to live by. He did not leave them to be placed in a glass cabinet like a relic in a museum. He did not leave them for a select group or an inner court – we know from Jesus' story exactly what he thought of those in ecclesiastical authority.

Jesus' words are a gift – and maybe a frightening burden too – to us all. For those of us who want to see the Church healed, ours is the call towards replacing autocracy with authenticity. It is a call to be very brave in real faith. Such a Church, authentic to the simple teachings of those beatitudes, will allow those who are chosen to hold the particular roles of priest, bishop, cardinal and pope, to do so as true servants and not as masters or princes.

Minded by the laity, an authentic Church would not permit its office bearers to become themselves, victims of the system like salt that has lost its taste. Instead, they would be compassionate leaders, more akin to those they lead, than as strict and remote figures of authority.

A new unity between clergy and laity could be the antidote to the Church's current toxic culture. However, and here is the real challenge, this will require those who hold positions of privilege within the organisation to yield some of their power to others who can bring their skills into play for the good of the Church.

I've often felt that in describing its core creed as 'one, holy, catholic and apostolic' Church, the Catholic Church has shackled itself to itself. What I mean by that is that seeing itself in those terms has meant that it can't learn readily from other Christian traditions who have walked similar paths. Anglicanism and Presbyterianism both embrace such lay involvement as intrinsic to their culture. Catholicism – perhaps because it's so large and unwieldy, but I suspect it's because of its descriptor as the one true Church– has been left far behind. The lessons, though, are there to be learned from. The faithful, who love their Church, can be trusted to mind it well. It belongs to them, after all.

A New Vision of Priesthood
When institutions are ablaze, there is a tendency to retreat into memories of a halcyon past, when everything was simpler, safer and more comfortable. We see this in the

political sphere – a harkening back to the days when society seemed so much more at ease with itself, when people knew their place and when those born into privilege were destined to govern.

In the Catholic Church throughout the world, this way of thinking can be observed today. We are already seeing this in a new resurgence of a quest for certainty in some priests and bishops, not only in Scotland, but throughout the world. A certainty that we were a better Church when the altar rails – figurative and real – were present that kept the laity in their place and the priest in his. This thinking will lead to calamity for the Church. Being more shrill, more strident, more condemnatory, more 'clerical' is no answer. We've tried that.

If Keith O'Brien's story has taught us anything it is that the 'brotherhood of the priesthood'– its exclusivity and its failure to embrace equality – is a danger to the Church now.

The celibate, single sex priesthood needs to be dismantled. Celibacy is not a sacramental requirement for the priesthood. Celibacy is not Church *doctrine*. Having been imposed by the Second Lateran Council in 1139 it is Church *practice*. This distinction is highly significant. Having a single-sex priesthood and episcopacy has allowed many of the deep-rooted cruelties within Catholicism to become entrenched throughout the whole institution.

My own story attests to the fact that there is a heroic appeal in the sacrificial nature of 'giving it all up' for a higher, more noble cause. But for that to be an authentic choice, there needs to be a backdrop of many things. Amongst them is sexual and psychological maturity.

The ingrained distrust and fear of women, as human as well as sacramental equals to men, was built into the bricks of 'priestly formation'. As a result, it is little wonder when you look at many of the clergy running parishes right across the Catholic world, and the bishops running their dioceses, you see many misogynistic, emotionally immature and repressed men who cannot make sense of a modern world which is increasingly more equal, more diverse, and which questions their authority.

Single-sex organisations tend not to be the healthiest and most harmonious of places. Arguably if you are, say, running a men-only golf-club, people will scratch their heads and wonder at the sheer irrelevance of such a thing in modern-day society, but that is where it ends. Few people, if any, would become irrevocably damaged as a result of such an organisation.

The Church is a vastly different thing, though. It's the institution to which a billion people turn for spiritual support, comfort and guidance as they make their way through the tortured path of human existence. So why would we assume that it would be any healthier, any more authentic to its core values, if fifty percent of the population are excluded from holding the office of deacon, priest, bishop or pope because of their gender?

On 3 November 2019 three organisations (Voice of Faith, We are Church Ireland and The School of Religion in Trinity College) organised an event in Trinity College, Dublin under the banner 'The Women The Vatican Could Not Silence'.

Streamed worldwide and in front of an audience of 400 in the auditorium the event focused on a conversation between two of the modern Church's most eloquent and radical female voices: Sr Joan Chittister and former President of Ireland, Mary McAleese. It was a truly inspirational event for those who desire to see the Church move to embrace women into all levels of its governance.

At one point, when asked about her description of the role of women in the Catholic Church, Sr Jean Chittister responded with one word: 'invisible'. She went on to say how much she loved the Church, 'But at the same time,' she went on, 'someday you have to wake up. You have to ask what you are looking at. You have to say what you see. The Catholic Church, for women, is a totally owned subsidiary of pious males.' Women are the outer edge; the bow on the package.

Both women were asked by the facilitator why women can't be priests. Chittister's response made my spine tingle. 'It's the wrong question,' she declared. 'The question is single, it's basic, it's universal. It's the only one and it is: "Are women human?" And if women *are* human then they can do anything a human can do. They can be lawyers; they can raise their voices in operating rooms in hospitals. They can do anything. If you ask for the Church answer, you're going to get the Church answer. It's "no." If you ask for the human answer you must say "yes". And that's the question they will not permit to be applied to the Church.'

What does the Church answer look like in practice? At a local level, women might obtain some administrative positions within diocesan or parish structures, and they may hold some minor roles like Eucharistic ministers, and during Pope Francis' papacy there has been a slight move towards enhancing women's roles within various Vatican departments, but they are denied any place in the diaconate and of course the priesthood. In turn, parishes are denied the gift of ministry that women priests would bring to Catholicism. Would the Church be in the mess it's in if the Pope were a woman?

It was on the day of the referendum to repeal the 8th Amendment (which denied women the right to abortion in Ireland) of the Irish constitution, 25 May 2018, that I came across a poem that stopped me in my tracks, not just because of its potency, but also because it so eloquently summed up for me the role women have been forced to adopt within Catholicism as well as in wider society. It is by Angela Carr, a poet living and writing in Dublin.

Silently, the Women Waited

The clocks ticked down, the men debated
the Proclamation and celebrated
while, silently, the women waited

a hundred years to be placated,
a body, sovereign, emancipated –
the clocks ticked on, the men debated –

and by the roadside Virgin, consecrated,
and on ferry crossings, expediated,
silently the women waited

in convent laundries, incarcerated,
their 'fatherless' children emigrated –
the clocks ticked on and men debated

a beach and the infant excavated,
a corpse and the foetus incubated,
still, silently the women waited,

mental acuity checked and rated,
septicaemia equivocated:
the clocks ticked on, the men debated
and, silently, the women waited.

The poem speaks to me of the vast gulf that exists, not just in Irish civil society, between women and men in terms of political, bodily and sexual autonomy. This gulf is also a dominating and domineering presence in the Church. It demonstrates the gender apartheid that runs deep in the organisational DNA of the Catholic hierarchy. For as long as this is allowed to go unchallenged and unchanged, Catholicism can only ever teeter on the precipice of relevance. This is where we are. For Catholics it is a perilous place to be. It is a long drop down.

In my view, the issue of the exclusion of women from priestly ministry is one of fundamental civil rights. It is every bit as distorting and disfiguring as refusing the right to vote because of gender, colour, sexuality or class. It may well be that, as lay people, we need to adopt the peaceful outrage of the civil rights movement in order to bring about change, if those in ecclesiastical power refuse to listen and adapt.

The nature of Christ's ministry, all that he spoke of in fact, is tenderness, forgiveness and compassion. He understood the law, but he knew that love transcends the law. The law itself could not contain or bind his message. So, when you hear the argument being used against the ordination of women that since Jesus only chose men to be his apostles, women therefore have no place in the priesthood, it simply reflects the cultural norm of Jesus' time, not the transcendent, true and authentic message of Jesus. That historical, cultural norm though is the default starting point for many in the brotherhood. It is embodied in men like the head of the Congregation for the Doctrine of the Faith, Cardinal Luis Ladaria, who was reported in *The Tablet* on 1 June 2018 as having said:

> the Church's belief in a male-only Priesthood is infallible teaching which should be held as an unchanging and 'definitive' part of the Catholic faith.' In the most forthright doctrinal statement so far against the ordination of women under Francis' papacy, the CDF Prefect says maleness is 'an indispensable element' of the Priesthood, and the Church is 'bound' by Christ's decision to choose male apostles.

It's worth pointing out that the Church has never declared the male priesthood to be infallible teaching. We can see that being a cardinal does not protect you from being mistaken.

But still, we have a long road to travel. There are many arguments to be made about the nature of being an apostle and a priest. The ties that bind the brotherhood are strong, but they are not all-powerful. They can be broken. They must be.

In the meantime, we have what we have. Priests are men, some with open hearts and minds; others with scars and fears. Some use their priesthood as a free pass to get their own way. Others still continue to walk their path humbly, trying their best to get through life's challenges. But it won't, it can't, continue like that. That's not enough.

In this respect (and in fact in many others) the Catholic Church has the opportunity to learn from other, reformed, Christian denominations. Women priests and bishops have been a long time coming in Anglicanism. But they're here. It could be that change is harder to bring about in the Catholic Church because it's so big, and old and creaky. But I sense an inevitability in this regard. If Catholicism needs ordained priests to carry out its ministry, and if there is a shortage of those priests, then opening Holy Orders to women, and the grace that that will bring, makes theological and practical good sense.

There is also something to be considered in how men (and in the future women) are prepared and trained for priesthood. On reflection, I think I would have had a much more rounded view of the priesthood if my development had been completely integrated into parishes like the one I attended in Ratho and if my studies had been undertaken at nearby Edinburgh University. Tertiary education is such a precious opportunity. It's easily squandered and, sadly, the intellectual and academic calibre of many of the profs who taught me in Drygrange was such that they probably would have found life hard as teachers in a university environment. But at the very least I'd have had a degree to show for my efforts.

We were told by the profs that the reason the cardinal at the time (Gordon Gray) did not want the seminary to offer a degree – apparently the degree awarding bodies were open to doing so – was to make it difficult for priests to later leave the priesthood. It was a calculated and cruel abuse of power from the very top of the Church in Scotland.

I also would have had a much better understanding of what being a priest actually meant away from the artificiality, with all that implies of an all-male environment. The model is evolving, with more integration into academic institutions happening now for those preparing for the priesthood. However, seminaries, in my view, serve no real purpose anymore, if they ever truly did. They are where power abuse is first displayed for future priests.

Misusing Power

How does the Church abuse its power?

Let's begin with a reflection on spiritual abuse based on my own experience. I have had a long number of years to reflect on the nature of O'Brien's ill-judged embrace at night prayer in his bedroom. He didn't rape me, but what he did was still abuse. That abuse of power was really what had the most lasting impact on me; I felt betrayed, and I felt something was stolen from me.

To try to describe what those consequences were for me, I need to take you back with me to Drygrange. When people asked me when I started in the seminary 'Why do you want to be a priest?' I would answer with some obtuse statement about feeling that God was calling me. It took me those first two years to build up what was even then still an unformed answer. I was really trying very hard to form a grown-up response.

Before entering the seminary I was just a wee Catholic boy from Fife. I knew religious words like Baptism, Holy Communion, Confession, Mortal Sin, Hell and Heaven. My knowledge of what it took to learn to be a priest was like a thin veneer of varnish over a six-inch block of wood. I wanted to be a priest, but I didn't know how to pray, and I didn't know what theology or religion was actually *for*.

However, rather than run for the hills in the face of those challenges, I tried my very best to meet them, and in my early times in Drygrange especially, I struggled every day. I cried real tears. I worried myself sick about passing my exams; about not making a fool of myself and letting others down. I tried, and then I tried harder. More than anything else I worried about being sent home, and what the consequences of that would be. Those first two years, despite being psychologically brutal in so many ways, were the beginning of me believing that I could begin to formulate a better answer to the question 'Why be a priest' than just 'Oh, I feel God is calling me'.

This emotionally immature and naïve adolescent was slowly beginning to feel confident in himself. I was beginning, taking baby steps, to assert myself; to claim an identity as a future priest. I was beginning to frame what that actually meant: the desire to be a servant, to seek out those whom society rejects. These became the ever more identifiable reasons why I was becoming a priest. During those first two years I developed a dawning awareness of Catholic Church social teaching on issues like nuclear weapons and liberation theology in Latin America. I never knew about any of that before Drygrange.

More than anything else I had found the raw intellectual stimulation that came through the study of moral theology: finding the tools, the critical thinking and the pathways to argue that what many see as the 'black-and-white' teaching of the Church on matters such as sex or medical ethics, were in fact more nuanced than I had first perceived. All those layers of Catholic theology were being peeled away and I was becoming equipped with ways of thinking and the language to argue and to persuade.

But all of that was predicated on the firm belief that others, and particularly my friend and spiritual director, Keith O'Brien, would help me on this journey by imparting what they knew, and set an example to emulate, by the way they lived their lives. When I sat down in the chapel that Saturday morning after he had abused my trust in him, and looked at O'Brien's gaunt, haggard face, it felt as though the whole edifice had come crashing down; that the man who had inspired me in my studies and in my personal development on the road to priesthood had betrayed me in the most cynical way possible. I remember feeling the death of something that morning. Not surprisingly, perhaps, this moment of profound crisis also neutralised for me the notion of prayer as a sacramental or supernatural communion with the Divine for many, many years. O'Brien must have known when a young man who can't pray, but needs to pray, tells him of his difficulty, then that young man is in a very vulnerable place indeed.

As the decades passed, and I heard how O'Brien had abused other priests, I often asked myself how he could live with himself, how he could sleep at night knowing that he had caused so much harm yet still confidently stride the ecclesiastical stage as an archbishop and a cardinal.

I think I might have a partial answer to that question. It lies in a very strange encounter I had with O'Brien many years after I left the priesthood. I had taken to going to mass again, not every Sunday, but fairly often, and had been convinced by my then parish priest that I should regularise my sacramental life with the Church and seek a dispensation from my priestly vows. This would mean I could be a practicing Catholic again. This process is called laicisation.

As part of this process one thing I was told I would have to do by the priest in charge of the process would be to have a face-to-face meeting with O'Brien in Edinburgh. It would be an understatement to say that I was not looking forward to it, but eventually the day arrived and I found myself, after a space of thirty or so years, at St Benet's, the Cardinal's mansion. In response to my knock, the housekeeper answered the door and explained that His Eminence was conducting a media interview and that I was to wait in the housekeeper's parlour. After about fifteen minutes, in he walked.

He still had his laughter lines round the eyes and the same lilt in his voice, but I was surprised by how much he had aged – how unsteady he was, how frail he looked. He asked to sit close beside me because his hearing was not good.

In the intervening years my feelings about him had hardened – not just because of what he had done to me but also because what he'd written or said relating to Church teaching, especially on sexual and ethical matters. Now I found myself sitting next to him, my coldness towards him began to slowly thaw, and our initial mutual frostiness fairly soon dispersed. It wasn't what I'd describe as a warm meeting, but when he said that he'd do what he could to expedite my laicisation, I knew we'd gained some common understanding. At the same I also felt strongly that he was measuring me up; that he trying to assess what reasons I might give for asking to be laicised, and whether any of them might have a direct impact on him.

Our conversation turned to Drygrange. I brought up the incident of the odd-job man's birthday cake and the re-igniting candles. I was amazed that he remembered it. He laughed hard. He still saw it as a harmless and humorous incident. I told him that I really thought I'd be thrown out for my role in the prank, but because he had told me to do it I had been saved. His response chilled me: 'They were angry with me too, but I can do what I want now.'

I felt my throat constricting. In that single phrase O'Brien disclosed to me what he felt about his place in the Church. 'I can do what I want now.' Corruption in the Catholic Church – or in any organisation – begins with men and women who can confidently utter such words. He was to find out – through a seemingly random turn of events and in just a few short years – that he could not, in fact, do what he wanted. None of us can.

I announced that I had to be going and I'd need a taxi to take me to the bus station. We went to the outer hall of St Benet's. He showed me various photos around the wall as we waited. This was the hall I'd waited in to be interviewed by O'Brien's predecessor prior to my admission to Drygrange all those years ago. Eventually the doorbell rang. It was time to go. He embraced me and pulled me towards him with an intensity, an intimacy. He brushed his cheek next to mine. I felt his old man's bristles. I was instantly transported back to our spiritual direction sessions.

Tears welled up in my eyes. After all those years, the hurt bubbled through. They were tears for myself. They were tears for the wasted years, wasted opportunities, and a wasted education during which instead of reading eschatology I could have been reading Graham Greene. I decided at that moment I would not participate in the technical process of laicisation. I realised that I did not need Church approval to lead my own best life.

It might be argued that this spiritual abuse has been made manifest more and more clearly through the clerical sex abuse crisis. For many of us as Catholics we have been brought up to regard the priest as an entirely benign and welcome presence. Deep within Catholicism lies the shadowy presence of clericalism – the promotion of the clergy as sort of holy superheroes with special powers and a slightly awe-inspiring presence. Clericalism tends to be thought of as something priests are guilty of – seeing themselves as better or more important as lay people in matters concerning the Church. But often laity themselves are guilty of clericalism. Think of the titles we give our clergy. I now see no reason to call a priest 'Father', a bishop 'Your Grace', a cardinal 'Your Eminence' or a pope 'Holy Father'. Some may see this as a trivial point of semantics. I don't believe it to be. How we behave as lay people to the clergy and the hierarchy must be as equals showing maximum respect for our equality in the eyes of God. We need cultural and behavioural, as well as spiritual and theological, reformation within the Church.

One of the mistakes that I made in my seminary formation was to conflate my faith in the Divine with my idolatry of O'Brien. I don't beat myself up about it: I was young and naïve. But it's still going on throughout Catholicism and it must be challenged. For sure, priests and bishops and cardinals and popes have caused the abuse of power within Catholicism by their actions. But the laity have allowed themselves to become awestruck and infantilised by the aura of the clergy. This is what happens when we don't mind the Church carefully.

Another type of power abuse lies within the bureaucracy of the Church. I've highlighted earlier that almost guttural feeling I got when I knew I was being ignored. The silence from the Nuncio, the lack of response from Cardinal Ouellet, the lack of acknowledgement from the pope. But I've seen it, too, in the health service on the back of the bullying complaints.

It's the off-handedness that they know, but don't care, that causes so much offence.

News broke of O'Brien's predation towards his priests in 2013. Seven years later the Social Care Institute for Excellence delivered an audit into how the archdiocese of St Andrews and Edinburgh was handling safeguarding issues in the light of the global shock and outrage at O'Brien's behaviour. With a new Archbishop, Leo Cushley and, I'm sure, the fulsome backing of the Vatican to make improvements it seems like an impossibility that this could fail.

The audit didn't skirt around the bush in laying out some of the diocese's challenges. Talking about the challenge of assuming leadership where there was a high-profile case of clergy abuse the report states:

> A change of leadership creates the possibility to focus on restorative practice as it offers an approach to:
> • help all affected parties come to terms with the facts, the betrayal and the possibility of their own, albeit unwitting, part in allowing abusers to go unchecked; and

- to identify and righting any wrongs of the past, working closely and compassionately with survivors to hear and respond to what they need. (2.1.28)

It then points out the particular challenge that the incestuous nature of the brotherhood of the priesthood brings with it.

It is challenging, however, when the prominent member of senior clergy has formed close working relationships and friendships with many in the Diocese, when survivors and others past efforts to bring the abuse to light have not been responded to appropriately and there is inevitable loyalty to your predecessors. (2.1.29)

The power of the brotherhood brings with it silence, secrets and omertà. The report talks about O'Brien's charisma, generosity and informality. All factors which made acceptance of the damage he did to individuals hard to accept. Which may explain why so many questions remain unanswered.

O'Brien volunteered to retire, and this was accepted by the Pope. He was not accused of crimes but of an abuse of power and there has been no criminal prosecution nor canonical disciplinary measure. The report or conclusions of the Vatican's investigation have never been published. The extent of O'Brien's alleged predatory sexual behaviour remains unclear, as does his alleged promotion or punishment of individuals according to how they responded to his advances, whether his clergy colleagues knew or suspected that O'Brien was abusing others, whether there had been any previous attempts to escalate concerns or whistleblow and whether secrecy about homosexuality contributed to the cover- up of abuse. (2.1.33)

Yet it appears that little effort has been made by O'Brien's successor, Leo Cushley, to even try to answer them:

The current Archbishop, on assuming his role, spoke of the need for reconciliation and healing within the church in Scotland. The audit suggests that there is still much to do in achieving this goal. In the face of the challenges detailed above, there remains an outstanding and pressing need for courageous, constructive leadership to foster open conversations about the actions of Keith O'Brien and what the position is of senior leaders in the Archdiocese to such abuses of power, and such hypocrisy. (2.1.35)

Indeed, the report goes on to ask a series of very probing questions of Cushley and his senior team:

Questions for the Archdiocese to consider:
• How does the Archdiocese plan to provide self and wider parish reflection and resolve following the O'Brien case? Have efforts to secure transparency about the facts of the O'Brien case in order to support learning been adequate?

• Can more be done to secure transparency about the facts of the O'Brien case in order to support learning, been adequate?

• How can the Archdiocese enable learning for clergy and laity regarding the distinction between being sexually active and an abuse of power?

• Are there plans to use the Independent Inquiry into Childhood Sexual Abuse in Institutional Settings (IICSA) report on Church of England Chichester Cathedral to draw out how secrecy about homosexual relationships can inadvertently enable the abuse of children?'

The report is a devastating read for those of us who have worked hard for the truth about O'Brien to be told and, crucially, for the Church to learn from its mistakes. Again and again, as I have made my way through the audit, I'm left with one abiding thought: that these men of privilege, feted for their rank, believe that it will all just magically disappear. A 'minding' laity can and must never allow such power abuse to go unchecked.

I remember I asked one high-ranking official about the progress that Scicluna had made with his report, as the whistleblowing priests had heard nothing for months. 'It is in the hands of others,' he said. My response of 'Well, can't you ask and find out for me?' was met with a thin-lipped 'That's not how things work in this organisation.' The same man had spent a number of years working in the offices and corridors of the Vatican. He made an impact on me, but probably not in the way he intended when he said, with a shrug, 'I once had power, but now I am a mere archbishop . . .'

And of course, he's right. It's about power. That is what, at the end of the day, many of them seek or have thrust upon them. It must be very hard to resist, no matter how kind and prayerful and intelligent you might be, the distorting impact that the power of the Catholic Church brings on men appointed to such positions.

* * *

I dreamt about Drygrange for a long time after I departed the priesthood. A recurring one was of me walking towards and then standing outside O'Brien's room. Just standing. Waiting. I thought somehow that if I went back to visit the place, I might put them to rest; they were exhausting me.

The building had been sold by the archdiocese in 1986 and was now a residential home for elderly people. I phoned, asking if I could come to visit my old college. A friend and I were shown round. The only part which had not been visibly altered was the new wing where I had spent my first year, and we asked to be taken up there. No elderly residents were housed there, and the rooms were empty.

It was a curious feeling walking those corridors, and memories whizzed through my mind. Seminarians' laughter, prayers and sobs now caught in the echoes of time. But first we headed for the chapel, and almost magically I caught a whiff of the floor polish that I had lovingly applied all those decades past.

Then we crossed the enclosed bridge connecting the original house to the new wing and walked up the flights of stairs to the room where I had stayed. I paused outside the door of my old room. This was the door too of the room the young man had lived in who killed himself. I turned the handle and walked in. The bookcase was empty, there was no bed. But it was my room. Strangely though, it was thick with dead flies. Clearly the door had been closed for months if not years and generations of them had bred and died in there.

I looked quickly out of the window. I remembered when I had been studying long into the night for an essay due in the next day. It was on Church heresies. I think I was struggling with a particular phenomenon called Jansenism. The Jansenists were a miserable lot – their main concern being the depraved nature of the human condition. I remember looking out into the dark of the night having been distracted by the lights of a car. I had taken my brown Anglepoise reading lamp and flicked the switch on and off in the direction of the receding lights. Dot-dot-dot, dash-dash-dash, dot-dot-dot, I signalled. Save-Our-Souls.

The dreams did fade. Over time.

* * *

My final reflection on the misuse of bureaucratic power lies with the notion of 'moral maturity' in those with whom this power lies. It is best demonstrated in Scotland through a story that became known following the news of O'Brien's sexual predation becoming public.

The Bishops' Conference is a term used to describe the organising structure of bishops in a specific area. It allows them to undertake coordinated work across various dioceses.

Cardinal O'Brien was the president of the Scottish Bishops' Conference during his term of office.

The example is about how the Conference of Bishops in Scotland behaved around a simple issue associated with auditing cases of paedophilia by priests. This was not about punishing paedophile priests who raped children. It was essentially calculating how many child-abusing priests were, or had been, on the books. Not a difficult job, nor particularly controversial.

On 24 August 2013, Mario Conti, Emeritus Archbishop of Glasgow, wrote a letter to *The Tablet* in which he responded to a previous piece critical of the Scottish Church around the issue of child sex abuse by clergy. This was after the news of O'Brien's sexual misdemeanours became known to the public. In it he made this surprising disclosure:

> It was the intention of all but one member of the bishops' conference to commission an independent examination of the historical cases we had on file in all of our respective dioceses and publish the results, but this was delayed by the objection of the then-president of the conference; without full participation of all the dioceses the exercise would have been faulty.

REACTION TO THIS DECISION WAS SWIFT.
THE BBC REPORTED
'Writing to the Tablet, Emeritus Archbishop of Glasgow Mario Conti said Cardinal O'Brien, who has admitted sexual misconduct with other priests, prevented the investigation.

Other Scottish bishops had agreed the inquiry should go ahead.

However, the Catholic paper's deputy editor said the church should have proceeded with an audit anyway. Elena Curtis said: "Cardinal O'Brien was one bishop and there would have been no reason why the other bishops couldn't have proceeded with an independent audit without him."

Alan Draper, an academic who was appointed in mid-1990s to advise the Church on sexual abuse and how to respond to it, said he was surprised by Archbishop Conti's claims.

"What does that tell you about the other bishops? Where is their personal integrity?

"Were they not prepared to say 'the survivors and victims are demanding these sorts of reviews', we're going ahead with it?

"Until they do that, they'll continue to have very low credibility among the laity.""

Of course, had they chosen to, the bishops could have published the incomplete audit. But they actively chose not to do so. I do not believe it was merely because the 'exercise was faulty' as Conti claimed. It was more likely because they did not want to be embarrassed by the fact that one of their number – the most senior of their group – decided that he wasn't up for it. Knowing something of the power of the Church I can understand that reluctance. They too have had to work in ways that they never imagined they'd have to, when they told their parents that they wanted to be priests.

This is what organisations with their backs to the wall do. They compose strategies that avoid the public gaining an insight into how they really operate. They rely on the meekness of the laity not to challenge them, and when one of their number is weakened they point the finger and say 'it was him. He made us do it.'

This is an example where we, as Catholics or people interested in Catholicism, must set aside our belief that 'they' will fix it for us. If the 'they' is the bishops and the hierarchical masters of the Church, we must surely now realise that to be true leaders we need spicy people in charge. Many of our bishops are like salt that has lost its flavour. That they cling on to power by virtue of their rank, rather than the merit of their actions, is unacceptable given the damage that they have caused.

Misunderstanding Sex

Two comments from O'Brien stand out when they are seen side by side: 'I can do what I want now' And following the whistleblowing into his sexual predation: 'I wish to take this opportunity to admit that there have been times that my sexual conduct has fallen below the standards expected of me as a priest, archbishop and cardinal.'

Power and Sex. What a heady brew.

That second statement begs a number of questions. The main one for me is: what is acceptable sexual conduct for a priest, archbishop or cardinal?

I think we have to start from the premise that we all have a sexual aspect to our lives. Even the Pope has a sex life. Mother Theresa? Jesus? Of course. The sexual part of our beings is as intrinsically important to our lives as any other biological part.

In 1975 the Church produced a decree called *Persona Humana*. It recognised that sexuality is central to being a human on many different levels: biological, psychological and spiritual. However, the decree then goes on to pronounce:

> In moral matters man cannot make value judgments according to his personal whim: In the depths of his conscience, man detects a law which he does not impose on himself, but which holds him to obedience . . . For man has in his heart a law written by God. To obey it is the very dignity of man; according to it he will be judged. [Section 3]

Sex and sexuality is no free for all, declares the Church. It's governed by a divine law that lies deep within the very core of human beings. When our time comes, we'll be judged accordingly to that law, we're told.

Let us apply a short analysis to O'Brien's statement to understand it in the light of what the Church itself teaches. When Church officials issue statements like the one O'Brien did, every single word will have been considered and calibrated by very senior authorities in the Vatican. Every nuance will have been tested. This would not have been the time for any loose language.

The key word O'Brien uses is 'standards' – the standards expected of priests, archbishops and cardinals. He doesn't explain those standards in detail as they applied to his own behaviour. However, he did outline what those standards were elsewhere when he used his platform as archbishop to condemn behaviour at odds with Catholic teaching.

The *Independent* newspaper on 15 May 2013 declared 'He was an outspoken critic of homosexuality, which he had called a "moral degradation".' This was also reported in *Vanity Fair* on 15 November 2013 in a fascinating article entitled 'The Vatican's Secret Life' by Michael Joseph Gross. In a very telling, and in the light of subsequent events extremely risky, statement he is quoted in America, *The Jesuit Review* on 19 March 2018 about homosexual priests: 'He also had said the presence of homosexuals in the Priesthood is not a problem "if they are leading a celibate life".'

Almost a year to the day before the story about his own hypocrisy was exposed O'Brien wrote an article for the *Daily Telegraph* (3 March 2012) and was forthright in his stance against same sex marriage:

> This is a point of view [that marriage can only take place between a man and a woman] that would have been endorsed and accepted only a few years ago, yet today advancing a traditional understanding of marriage risks one being labelled an intolerant bigot.

Lest we think that no-one takes seriously words like these, we need to be reminded that on 7 March 2012 *The Scotsman* reported on some of the reaction to O'Brien's proclamations.

> The cardinal's controversial stance was yesterday praised by those close to the Zimbabwean president [Robert

Mugabe] who has argued that homosexuals are 'worse than pigs and dogs', as well as using the issue of gay rights to attack the West and opposition parties that back same-sex unions.

There was also strong support for the cardinal from Zimbabwean clerics, with one church leader in the crisis-torn African nation saying: 'He is like a Martin Luther who had a revelation and has been inspired to get the truth.'

He didn't limit himself to homosexuality and gay marriage in his bluster. *The Guardian* reported his eye-watering condemnation of abortion on 1 June 2007 which he likened to 'two Dunblane massacres a day.' (The Dunblane massacre referenced took place on 13 March, 1996 in the tiny village near Stirling in Scotland. Thomas Hamilton shot 16 children and a teacher dead before killing himself.)

In 2008 his aim was at politicians, describing the Human Embryology and Fertilisation Bill being discussed as 'monstrous' and an endorsement of experiments of 'Frankenstein proportions'. The *Daily Telegraph* which ran the report on 21 March 2008 noted that O'Brien's comments were 'the most vitriolic to date' amongst Catholic leaders.

One thing we can be absolutely sure of, with this cursory review of his pronouncements, was that O'Brien was very knowledgeable of Church ethical 'standards'. Maybe more pertinent to O'Brien's own life was that he also knew the Church's teaching on what are called 'intrinsically evil acts'. All priests, and most Catholics, know this bit.

Here's what *Persona Humana* (section 8) spells out (this time I cannot spare you the magisterial tone):

> homosexuals must certainly be treated with understanding and sustained in the hope of overcoming their personal difficulties and their inability to fit into society. Their culpability will be judged with prudence. But no pastoral method can be employed which would give moral justification to these acts on the grounds that they would be consonant with the condition of such people. For according to the objective moral order, homosexual relations are acts which lack an essential and indispensable finality. In Sacred Scripture they are condemned as a serious depravity and even presented as the sad consequence of rejecting God. This judgment of Scripture does not of course permit us to conclude that all those who suffer from this anomaly are personally responsible for it, but it does attest to the fact that homosexual acts are intrinsically disordered and can in no case be approved of.

This is explained further in another Church document, *Veritatis Splendor*, authored by Pope John Paul II in 1993: 'These are the acts which, in the Church's moral tradition, have been termed 'intrinsically evil' (*intrinsece malum*)'(Number 80).

None of this teaching would have been news to O'Brien. Whether he agreed with them or not, these teachings are branded on the heart of every ministering (and non-ministering) Catholic priest. It is in the knowledge of this backdrop that we must interpret O'Brien's judgement on others, and on his own sexual behaviour.

According to Church teaching, perpetrating an intrinsically evil act entails serious sin. The more serious the act, the more serious the sin. These sins are known in the Church as 'mortal sins'. For Catholics, mortal sins need to be confessed and absolved by a priest because one's very soul is in peril.

When we are considering what O'Brien actually meant when he stated, 'I wish to take this opportunity to admit that there have been times that my sexual conduct has fallen below the standards expected of me as a priest, archbishop and cardinal', what he was applying was the harsh judgement that Catholic Church teaching applies to gay sex.

Was his statement a conscious attempt by him to reflect on his own behaviour and to appeal to his own self to become a better man? Possibly. But I'm sorry to say, I doubt it.

One of the clusters of sadness in all of this is that I do suspect that O'Brien's words will have left many listening and internalising them, in suffering and in pain. Women who have had abortions being somehow linked to a mass murderer; gay and lesbian couples being told that their expressions of love are abhorrent; politicians and scientists who seek to cure illness, as monstrous. How far removed are these expressions from the teachings of Jesus? How ill placed is the Catholic Church to judge what is and is not an acceptable sexual ethic?

In his book *In the Closet of the Vatican: Power, Homosexuality, Hypocrisy*, Frédéric Martel makes the following observation on pp. 9–10:

An Italian Benedictine monk, who was one of the senior officials at the Sant'Anselmo University in Rome, explained the logic to me: 'For me the choice of the priesthood was at first the product of a deep and vital faith. But retrospectively I also analyse it as a way of keeping my sexuality under control. I've always known that I was gay, but it was only later, after the age of 40, that I accepted this fundamental aspect of my identity'.

The priesthood of course has long been a natural home for gay men, especially in times when openness about one's homosexuality could lead to all sorts of opprobrium. According to Martel it doesn't stop at the decision to enter the priesthood: 'To this sociological selection of priests we might add the selection of bishops, which amplifies the phenomenon still further.' He goes on to explain how this occurs. 'Nuncios, those ambassadors of the pope who are given the task of selecting bishops and among who the percentage of homosexuals reaches record levels, in turn operate a 'natural' selection. According to all the statements that I have collected, the priests who have such inclinations are thought to be favoured when their homosexuality is guessed.'

He concludes: homosexuality becomes more prevalent the closer one gets to the holy of holies – there are more homosexuals as one rises through the Catholic hierarchy. In the College of Cardinals and at the Vatican, homosexuality becomes the rule, heterosexuality the exception.

In and of itself, the fact that there are so many homosexual men in the Vatican is neither here nor there. The trouble comes if they fail to maturely embrace their own sexual identity and consequently use their rank to demonise gay sex in the cruellest of ways. Describing gay expressions of love as 'intrinsically evil' being a case in point.

Where there should be a recognition of the ancient and highly honourable role that gay clergy (who struggle with celibacy just as much as straight clergy) have played in the active life of the Church across the centuries up until today, they are instead hounded and vilified. Their oppression is a source of shame on the Church. It is, as we've observed, also deeply hypocritical.

Embracing Our Human Frailty

There are increasing numbers of high-profile examples the misuse of power and sex and secrecy in the higher echelons of the Catholic Church. What happened to me at the hands of O'Brien is as nothing compared to the harrowing experience of many people who have suffered from clerical abuse and cover up.

I confidently predict that the Church will see more and more of these stories unfolding as the years and decades pass. Already there is a growing recognition of women in Religious orders, nuns, who are reporting having been systematically raped by male clergy. Some, who have become pregnant as a result, have been forced to undergo abortions in an attempt to cover up the situation.

So how does the Catholic Church allow such behaviour to continue? To answer that, we need to talk about sin.

I bristle when I hear the phrase 'hate the sin, love the sinner'. It was a phrase supposedly coined by St Augustine of Hippo. I used to hear it a lot after I left the priesthood and worked in the field of AIDS awareness and care in Edinburgh and in the Scottish Highlands.

As we've seen, the Catholic Church has a codified, hierarchical notion of sin. Sins for the Church are normally understood as evil actions related to, yet distinct from, their intention. One example of this was drummed into us in our theological training in the seminary. It probably won't surprise anyone, given the community we were in, to know what the example was.

The moral weight of the sin of masturbation is equally as bad if the intention is to produce sperm for infertility treatment (you might think that this would be a good act in a marriage – in order to have children) than it is because you were sexually aroused (by watching pornography, for example). Different intention, but the act is just as wrong in each case. The act leads to the sin. Back in the day, people would warn you not to put yourself in an 'occasion of sin'. However, if you go to Confession (the sacrament of Reconciliation) with a priest, your sins are absolved – they are washed away. That's what O'Brien did during spiritual direction. But, whilst he washed away my sins, he could not wash away my *sinfulness*. This is an important distinction.

The most opportune time for a Catholic to die is at the precise moment after leaving the Confessional, having received absolution for all the sins they have committed. It's why many Catholics wish to be absolved from their sins when on their death bed. The Church teaches that having received your Confessional shower, newly cleansed and in a state of grace, you go directly to heaven.

Having been on both sides of the grille, the truth is that Confession can be a purifying and healing experience. It is a very humbling thing for a priest to hear people talk of their pain and regret, and to look for a new beginning. The problem with Confession, however, as it's often practised, is that it fails to encourage deeper reflection, particularly with regard to what the Church defines as sexual 'sins'. Formulaic questions ('How many times?', 'Were you alone or with others?'), an almost fetishisation of sexual acts and the inevitable absolution, risk infantilising rather than maturing us. It allows us to feel free of the consequences of our acts because we are 'forgiven' through absolution.

The prospect of absolution would allow me, if I were an archbishop so inclined, to have sex with priests who are in awe of me and of my power over them. I could wake up in angst at what I had done, and in truth and humility seek Confession and Absolution. I could then in all solemnity, and full of grace, consecrate Communion wafers into the real presence of Christ and distribute them to the faithful. My sermon could include a rebuke, in the strongest terms, to the promiscuous world we live in.

Seán Fagan, a Marist priest in Dublin, wrote about such matters in his book *What Happened to Sin?* In one gloriously poetic passage he sums this topic up masterfully:

> Thus, we saw how narrow and crippling is the influence of an over-simplified notion of moral law; a preoccupation with precise measurement; a disproportionate concern with sexuality, particularly physical actions, without reference to their full human meaning;

judgement of isolated bits of behaviour divorced from the overall pattern of moral living; an inflated and morbid super-ego taking the place of conscience; neurotic guilt feelings smothering the experience of real moral guilt; the punishment of sin seen in terms of an angry, vengeful God; the sacrament of reconciliation used mainly as a guilt-shedding process with little experience of real conversion; the notion of God's forgiveness as something to be worked for and earned rather than accepted and celebrated as healing gift; morality presented simply as rules to be obeyed; unthinking conformity praised as obedience; the teaching authority of the Church used simply as power to command; the over-protective caution of those in authority, bishops, priests, teachers, parents; the failure to raise the level of people's reasoning about moral issues; the reluctance to promote autonomous moral decision; the lust for clarity and certainty beyond what is possible or appropriate. (p. 211)

Lying behind Fr Fagan's quote is another story. An inescapably sad one. But one which demonstrates the tyranny of the Church hierarchy at any sort of dissent like this. Mary McAleese, writing in *The Irish Times* on 17 July 2016, following Fr Fagan's death, tells it well:

A brilliant theologian and thinker who brought great distinction to Ireland, his long and illustrious priestly career was blighted in latter years by being silenced by the Congregation for the Doctrine of the Faith. His heart and spirit were broken but his fidelity to the

Church and quiet acceptance of such an unjust fate won him even more admirers,' she said. 'When, thanks to Pope Francis, the CDF finally restored him to good standing in 2014 it was a case of too little too late. A great and good man's life and his life's work had been ruined. Anyone wishing to comprehend the collapse of the Catholic intellectual tradition need only examine Seán Fagan's tragic story'.

It's my belief that confession must lead us to be better sinners who will never be free from our flawed state. This is our lot in life. We can always be better than we are.

There is something else though that the O'Brien case has opened up. Again it relates to Confession. I mentioned it earlier. What happens when this most intimate of encounters is exploited and abused? In the wake of the O'Brien scandal, John McLellan wrote in the *Edinburgh Evening News* (22 March 2018):

> The Church hierarchy was stunned to learn he had forced some of the Priests to hear his confession in which he admitted abusing them. It was a clerical means to gag the Priests for ever with the absolute secrecy of the confessional. Sexual relationships with Priests were bad enough, but it is another thing entirely for such a senior cleric to violate the sanctity of rites at the heart of its doctrine.

Mr McLellan is absolutely correct. I'm not sure, though, if it is fully understood by Catholics, or other interested parties, quite how serious this violation of Confession actually is. Unfortunately, we are dealing with some complicated theology. To spare you the ins and outs of canon law on this matter I'll sum up what it all means, and I'll cite the relevant codes or 'canons' at the end for anyone wishing to follow them up.

The Church takes a very dim view indeed of abuse of the sacrament of confession by priests or bishops to procure or cover up sex abuse. In short it is absolutely forbidden for priests to absolve one another for having had sex together. This is to avoid turning confession into a sort of circular sin/forgiveness racket

What's the penalty? Immediate excommunication of the offending parties. It's a theological concept called *excommunicatio latae sententiae.* What that means is that from the moment that the abuse of the sacrament of confession takes place that priest, bishop, or cardinal is excommunicated (in other words excluded from Church life in this world and from salvation in the next.) There are no forms to fill in, no process, no trips to Rome. It just happens. Only the Pope can revoke excommunication *latae sententiae.* For the avoidance of doubt, an excommunicated person can neither receive nor administer the sacraments.

If O'Brien had misused the sacrament of confession with fellow clergy, and there seems to be an understanding that he may have, then he will have been automatically excommunicated. What does the mean for all the marriages he conducted, the last rites he anointed, the confirmations he carried out, the eucharists he celebrated? What about all the priests he ordained? All of those sacraments would have been carried out illicitly. Does that mean that those people aren't *really* married or those men aren't *real* priests? The answer in short is 'no'. There is a difference in Catholic theology between a sacrament being 'valid' and 'licit'

Once again there are mountains of theology and philosophy which explain the difference. But essentially, what it means is that at his ordination to the priesthood a man is changed within his very being for ever. Indelibly. The term is 'ontological change'. So a priest can never *not* be a priest. Even an excommunicated priest, or bishop, is always a priest. Therefore, the specific functions that priests carry out – the administering of the sacraments – are always valid even if they are illicit.

There is no escape from this important teaching in canon law, and as a result perhaps thousands of Catholics may have received sacraments illicitly through Cardinal O'Brien. I may be one of them. And of course, as a cardinal, O'Brien would have been expected to understand and apply this aspect of canon law to himself as well as to others.

You might be wondering if this matters. Well, it only matters if you embrace such notions of valid and illicit sacraments. But they do form part of Catholic Church law. If I was a priest who was ordained by O'Brien illicitly then, at the very least, I would like to know about it. He didn't ordain me. But all those confessions. All those absolutions.

The matter raises other puzzles. In the scenario that O'Brien did abuse the Sacrament of Confession and was excommunicated automatically, and if the Vatican did nothing about it, O'Brien would have died in excommunication. That is a curious concept indeed given the implications for him when he meets his maker.

Of course, insofar as O'Brien apologised in a very general manner, if he told the Vatican about his abuse of the Sacrament of Confession and accompanying automatic excommunication, the Vatican would have been able to revoke that excommunication. Did that admission, repentance, and revocation occur? If so, the revocation of excommunication would have been all very well for O'Brien. But what about the many laity who may have received illicit sacraments from him (especially considering the large numbers of sacraments of confirmation that bishops perform)? These laity would be 'sacramental victims', so to speak.

If all this occurred, did the Vatican 'fix' the illicitness of those sacraments quietly at a desk in Rome? And even if they did so, does the laity not have a right to know about it? I suppose you could liken it to a health system that has made an error in health reporting. Even though no physical harm was done the ethical thing would be to tell those affected what had happened.

(The relevant references are canon 290, canon 977, canon 1008, Catechism number 2357, canon 1314, canon 1324 and canon 1331.)

'The over-simplified notion of moral law' that Seán Fagan has presented and promoted by the practice of individual confession of sins and absolution, needs to be replaced with a more reflective practice on the nature of sinfulness and Christ's call to holiness through the promotion of general absolution in a group setting. (This in fact happens during an examination of conscience at the start of every mass. But it's downplayed presumably in case it impacts on numbers going to individual confession.) This will allow those participating to focus less on the accounting practice of the number and type of sins they have committed, and more on their sinfulness in order to become better people and to develop their character.

Scandal and the People of God

Throughout this story, from Fr. Mackay through to Nuncio Mennini, avoidance of 'scandal' was the mood music. Perversely, the scandal wasn't really O'Brien's behaviour towards priests. That was secondary. The scandal was his behaviour becoming known by the laity and the outside world. This is a vital distinction. If we apply it to the wider paradigm of why bishops have covered up the actions of abusive priests by moving them to other parishes, rather than reporting them to the civil authorities, it becomes even more important that we take stock of this issue.

In his wonderful book 'Potiphar's Wife' Kieran Tapsell outlines in the clearest terms what 'scandal' means within the Catholic Church. Here's what he says:

> 'The word 'scandal' in the Church has a technical meaning beyond the usual. It means the loss of faith amongst the faithful when those who are supposed to act in the place of Christ, namely priests, bishops and religious, do the opposite.' P.52

> Tapsell goes on to outline how far the avoidance of scandal might reach:

> 'Catholic theology says that it is permissible to use 'mental reservation' to avoid 'scandal' and to preserve 'professional secrets'. Cardinal Desmond Connell, the

former Archbishop of Dublin explained 'mental reservation' to the Murphy Commission, as deceiving someone without telling a lie:

> ...there may be circumstances in which you can use an ambiguous expression realising that the person who you are talking to will accept an untrue version of whatever it may be....

> The sexual abuse of children of Priests [sic] was a 'scandal', and therefore it was possible to use 'mental reservation' to avoid it becoming public.' P.59

In an effort to reflect more on this I spoke to a senior clinical forensic psychologist friend of mine. I asked her if there were degrees of blame that could be ascribed to priests and bishops in the child abuse horrors. My hypothesis being that, arguably, the pedophile priest, whilst fully repugnant because of his rape and torture of innocent children, is, at the end of the day, believed to be suffering from a psychiatric condition. The bishops who hid them away...they were just callous bastards with no illness to defend them. 'That's right isn't it?'

My friend's answer floored me. In her warm, gentle style she opened up a new door that may be of interest to the Church. If it really wants to understand, and do something about the reasons why some priest sexually offend and why some bishops have let them do so on the basis of reducing scandal then the answer may well be found in how these men search out and meet their various 'primary needs' that I mentioned earlier.

We all have life goals: desires to be happy, to experience contentment in the world, to fulfil our creative potential. Most of us seek to achieve these goals in healthy ways.

But some don't. Some of these adored, but guarded priests, possibly with a range of psychological issues that the seminary system allowed them to cover up and lock tightly away, have done great wrong. A mix of maladaptive sexual maturity alongside status and privilege is a dangerous concoction.

The 'Good Lives Model' for offender rehabilitation is a very well recognised means of approaching offending behaviour. Essentially it recognises that all individuals have similar needs and aspirations. However criminal behaviour occurs when some individuals- priests who rape and abuse children for example – lack the resources to reach those needs in a manner that is healthy and prosocial. According to the Good Lives Model the best way to create a safer society is to help offenders to adopt more 'fulfilling and socially integrated lifestyles'.

But what about the bishops who covered for them though? Surely there can be no psychological theory to govern them covering up abusive priests? That's just sheer cowardice. Isn't it?

My friend said, 'I'd imagine the bishops were trying to meet some of their primary needs by the denial and covering up of abuse.'

Wait a minute! What? What primary needs could bishops have that even begin to explain away their behaviour?

'I suspect,' my friend said, 'there are similarities in the needs they were trying to meet, to the priests who did the abusing, which is why they were so effective.'

Priests and bishops are, by and large, intelligent men. Some are brilliant. They are used to adoration, but they are rarely challenged. In our society they live very comfortable middle class lives. Although they do not get a rich salary, certainly not in Scotland anyway, they tend to get a lot of gifts and money from parishioners.

For some of those bishops, being in power and in control may well be a primary need and the avoidance of scandal a means to achieve it.

While there are factors, some would argue supernatural factors ('ontological change'), that make priests and bishops different from others, at the end of the day, as my psychologist friend summed it up:

'People are people are people.'

And O'Brien was 'people' too. My friend's insight has gifted me a major tool to understand and find compassion for O'Brien and to answer the question why he behaved the way that he did.

Why live the double life? What were the primary needs that he felt he had to meet? Intimacy, power, romance, happiness? Possibly. He also needed the prestige that being a country's most senior catholic gave him. How he went about meeting those needs meant he had to make some serious moral compromises. Some of those compromises will have involved treating others poorly, trampling over them spiritually. Harming them.

The Church authorities, who cautioned us priests about going public about O'Brien, may have been genuinely concerned that people's very souls would be jeopardised if they lost their faith. These are heady, and potentially very toxic, reasons to justify cover up and subterfuge.

The fear of scandal and the primacy of protecting the reputation of the Church organisation has resulted in harm to victims of power and sexual abuse within the Church. The concept of 'scandal' is a distorting factor in decision making by those in powerful positions. It leads the Church away from the message and values of Jesus. It must be re-evaluated. Alongside this is the need for mature discussion on how the primary needs of priests are met. As I have said, one way might be dismantling the celibate and single sex model of priesthood and training these men in their craft in a much more nurturing way.

At the end of the day, the Church is a flawed institution, it always will be no matter how hard we reform it from within or from without. The best, most noble, aim we can have for it is the same as we can have for ourselves. Namely, keep reflecting, keep redefining, and keep drawing ourselves back to our core beliefs and values. At the moment the profound, heroic, kind Church is drowned out by the bombastic, misogynistic, self hatred of its hierarchy.

EPILOGUE:
WHERE DOES GOD HIDE?

Keith O'Brien died before this publication. I started writing this book when he was very much alive though. It started to become a serious proposition for me when I read some of the more destructive things he had to say particularly around same-sex marriage and abortion. With apparently little regard for the consequences of his words, O'Brien pounded on his pulpit like some form of Hibernian Calvinist, outraged by the sin and pestilence and sexual savagery he saw all round him, while at the same time he abused his power within his own circle of priests: those whom he had a special duty of care for, and his actions were in pursuit of his own self-indulgence. I don't believe that he ever thought that his words might hurt, damage, and potentially even end some lives. Even if he did he justified it to himself as being proportionate. Such was his certainty.

The Cardinal's Funeral Mass took place in the Church of St Michael in Newcastle on Thursday April 5th 2018 and not, as might be expected, in St Mary's Cathedral in Edinburgh. In death, as in the last five years of his life, Scotland's erstwhile most senior Catholic, was kept in exile by the order of Church authorities once news of his own sexual behaviour became public.

The Homily at his mass was preached by Cardinal Vincent Nichols, Archbishop of Westminster and he tried to to get the balance right.

'In recent days,' he said, 'the life of Cardinal Keith has been laid bare. We all know its lights and its darkness; we need not spend time talking about them even more for he has given us the key words. In his last will and testament he wrote: 'I ask forgiveness of all I have offended in this life. I thank God for the many graces and blessings he has given me especially the Sacrament of Holy Orders.' Today, as we pray for the repose of his soul, we also pray for all those he offended and ask God to strengthen them at this time.'

I'm sure another prayer was being said quietly and internally: 'let that be an end to it now. Let these be the last words'. But that can never be allowed to happen. For the Church to learn, we need to keep on reflecting on how we got to where we are.

If I had the opportunity to give the sermon at O'Brien's Funeral Mass myself, what would I have said?

I'd have addressed my words directly to him.

'We are a' Jock Tamson's bairns' at the end of the day, Keith. Despite our differences in status and the roads travelled we're united by one common reality: that we are all flawed. I'm no less a sinner than you.

There were many good things that you did with your life; good causes that you took up and championed. You showed kindness and humour in a world where such attributes are rare and required. You were a 'hands off' leader in the Archdiocese and generally didn't feel the need to police or micromanage parishes. You were unaligned to any movement or faction which controlled people's approach to the Church.

You were also a major influence in the direction of travel in my life. That life has ended up fine. But you did cause deep pain to many. When you wrote in your Will that you were sorry for those you 'offended', that word doesn't begin to address the damage that you did.

If forgiveness for the deep scars that have been caused to individuals and to Scottish Catholicism is required, then I for one, forgave you a long time ago. You were a wee boy once. Never in your wildest dreams would you have thought that your life would have taken the turns it did. You were a product of the poisoned, autocratic Church institution that brought you into its inner sanctum. And more than anything else, your actions, and the actions of countless other cardinals, archbishops, bishops and priests who have harmed others are the clearest argument for change in the Church that can ever be made. So let's bring about that reform . If we do then your legacy, in that regard, can be a rich one.

* * *

At the start of this book I wrote that this story was about three journeys. The first was my journey into and out of the priesthood. The second was the journey I made up close and personal with the pope's men. But the third journey – my personal one, into and out of belief. The aftermath. Where has that taken me?

Well…on every step of the way I have felt the pain, the rawness of my Ordination Scriptural Reading. It has become branded into me. It has shaped me and has scarred me. But it has been my story.

'My child, if you aspire to serve the Lord, prepare yourself for an ordeal.

Be sincere of heart, be steadfast, and do not be alarmed when disaster comes.

Cling to him and do not leave him, so that you may be honoured at the end of your days.

Whatever happens to you, accept it, and in the uncertainties of your humble state, be patient, since gold is tested in the fire, and the chosen in the furnace of humiliation.

Trust him and he will uphold you, follow a straight path and hope in him.

You who fear the Lord, wait for his mercy; do not turn aside, for fear you fall.'

Before he left my house, after our discussion, the Pope's emissary, Charles Scicluna told me something. I mean that literally. He told me something with a certainty that was at odds with our previous conversation.

He said 'And, Brian, there is a God.'

With these words he reached into the very core of my anxiety and distress. No other bishop or cardinal, had mentioned God throughout the entire process. Apart from the platitudes with which they signed off their letters. 'Yours in Christ'.

There is a God.

I have had many occasions to doubt that assertion throughout my life, and I have those doubts still. I don't let them bother me. I'll find out one way or the other in time.

My one certainty, as I've said, is that I am uncertain. But that declaration opened my frightened heart an inch or two to the possibility that it might be true: there might be a God. But that God lies well hidden – and is sometimes found in the most curious of places.

The End

ACKNOWLEDGEMENTS

Many people have helped me with this book. Some sources prefer to remain in the background. Their sharing of knowledge and wisdom has been remarkable. They know who they are and the importance they have in my life.

There are others whom I do want to mention. First amongst them are my priest friends who also suffered at the hands of Cardinal Keith O'Brien. Of course, I won't identify my fellow whistle-blowers. Their heroism in the face of so much pressure was a remarkable and humbling thing to observe. By not naming them, it does make it seem as though I was the only one on 'our side' who was doing any of the heavy lifting. I most definitely was not. I can only apologise to them if that's how it comes across. The Catholic Church throughout the world owes them, and every person who calls out power and sexual abuse by the clergy, a huge debt of gratitude. They changed things in Catholicism for the better. And they are the best of the priesthood.

The story was safely, skilfully and ethically brought to public awareness through the professionalism, personality and courage of the journalist Catherine Deveney. It was a complicated and high-profile story, and Catherine, together with the team at *The Observer,* brought it into the light of day for the world to read. What an incredible job she and they did.

Richard Holloway is someone I am honoured to have as a friend and a mentor. He has guided me with kindness, wisdom and great humour. He has kept me focused and taught me to keep pecking away when there was a temptation to run. I can never repay the debt I owe him.

A number of people have read and commented on the text as it has evolved and changed throughout the process. Donald MacLeod has walked the whole journey with me, forever positive and encouraging and gently challenging.

Therese Coffey, my dear friend from primary school, helped shape the book into a more comprehensive story and edited it with selflessness and great good humour. My friend and comrade Gavin Smith was so kind with his time and photographic skills in making the best of my image. Alyson Halcrow guided me in the early days of the Leith Group, and her friendship continues to be a great gift. My friend Samantha Cole has been a writing buddy to me and has read, re-read, and suggested changes with grace, kindness, patience and precision. Maura O'Toole carried out a detailed and so very helpful copy edit of the manuscript before I submitted it. A selfless act and I am utterly grateful.

There have been a group of people I have come to know extremely well as this book has progressed. Doctors who blew the whistle on the savage culture of bullying in NHS Highland over many years and people who, like me, worked to make sure justice was done for those who had been injured and harmed: Iain Kennedy, Jonathan Ball, Lorien Cameron-Ross, Al Miles, Chris Williams, Eileen Anderson, Alistair

Todd, Gavin Smith (again) and Linda Kirkland. People of true integrity and courage who have taught me how to be a better person.

I want to thank Garry O'Sullivan, Managing Editor of Columba Books, who believed in me and in 'Cardinal Sin'. He and his team have been a truly supportive and skilled presence in bringing my words to print. They made it happen.

And there are the many whose kindness, example, skill and encouragement have kept me going when I needed it most: Andrew Simmons, Allan, Ali and Teresa Thomson, Fiona MacAulay, Ken Walker, Rob Peel, Neena Jha, Jeannie Armstrong, Genevieve and Graham MacIver, Margaret and Fergus Ewart, the Keegans, Judie and Kevin Holliday, Valerie Hetherington and her extended family, Heather Tracey, Sophie Linington, Pip Farman, Jenye Monkton, Paul Hersee, Sherri Jackson and my Irish cousins Una Murray, Nora Montague and Mary Molloy. My funny, kind and sometimes crazy Twitter pals, and my friends in Ireland, Fife and here at home on the Black Isle.

It feels somewhat inadequate to thank the one person, Margaret Mary Clare (to use her full Sunday name), who has stood by me every step of the way. Words can't express what I feel for her. I'll stop trying to find them in the certainty that she knows what they are.

RELATED TITLE

ISBN 9781782183648

What happened to Fr Seán Fagan?
Angela Hanley

"Spill the beans in public on what really went on, to shame our sinful church in the hope that it might prevent further repetitions."

What happens when theologians are asked to obey rather than discover? Marist priest and theologian Fr Seán Fagan was widely admired and respected as a courageous and compassionate pastor. In 2010, he was censured by the CDF and forbidden from publishing or speaking in public about anything considered contrary to Church teaching. This book is Seán's opportunity to have his side of the story finally told.

columba
BOOKS